# ABOUT THE AUTHOR

David Gardner is a writer who spends his time travelling to beautiful parts of the world. He is a published author of books and scholarly articles and a bestselling author in travel writing.

David lives in Australia with his wife, children and a fluffball of a dog. His current passion is writing a series of travelogues from his journeys across the globe. He hopes you will share in his passion through these books and enjoy the journey.

## ACKNOWLEDGEMENTS

My heart-felt thank you to my wonderful wife, Wendy, who shares my trips, inspires me daily, infuses passion into everything we do and casts her critical eye over my work.

I would like to thank my good friends, Michael, for providing valuable feedback, and Ken, who has provided valuable proofing on this volume and been generous with his ideas for improvement. I would also like to thank my family and friends who put up with me and are always willing to read my work and make suggestions. Finally, I thank Igor Petkovski for the superb cover design.

# Cotswold Dreaming

A couple's 102-mile adventure along The Cotswold Trail

Book Two in the Gardner Travel Series

Knox Publishing

2018

David Gardner

Cover design: Igor Petkovski

# CONTENTS

## Escape

It was time to leave. Everyday life was grinding us down with its interminable demands. Groceries, bills, errands and maintaining a large house tend to kill the spirit if left unremedied for too long. Our spirit definitely needed renewal. Italy had once before provided the perfect antidote to that insidious disease called routine. This time, it would come in the form of a 102-mile walk along the beautiful Cotswold Way, in Southern England.

Wendy and I had been thinking about this particular remedy for quite a while. We were yearning for some *alone time*. Our first escape to Italy, now in a book titled *"White Roads and Red Wine: a couple's journey through Italy"* was possibly the most wonderful escape of our lives. This time, our dream of doing the Cotswold Way walk was a romp that would involve a good deal more adventure than we had bargained for.

The Cotswolds almost always tops the list when thinking of England's most desirable locations. Stories from our parents, TV shows and romantic films have reinforced it as a region of idyllic landscapes, quaint villages, and gentle charm. It regularly lays claim to the UK's most expensive real estate and the area in which many would like to live if they could afford it. It's not surprising. The region stretches across five English counties, all with low population density, an array of cultural attractions, excellent universities, natural beauty and boasting rich deposits of ancient history. Memory in this area reaches back to early Neolithic times. The counties have been home to our earliest ancestors, arriving from the Iberian Peninsula - the mysterious Celts, Romans, Saxons, and even Vikings, before eventually, the Normans came and conquered. Later, it became a region littered with castles and grand manors that have played roles in some of the country's most significant political and cultural events.

The Cotswolds is a region where you go to get away from it all. You can soak up its rural attributes and enjoy its unhurried lifestyle while only being a stone's throw from London. It's a place that captivates with its unique allure and seduces with elegant charm. But as we'll discover, it's also about far more than that.

Wendy insists on boarding our train at Paddington Station, London, so she can snap several dozen photos of the station's mascot Paddington Bear. We are heading for the quaint Cotswold village of Moreton-in-Marsh, which is a quiet and punctual one hour and thirty-minute train trip through country-side that belongs to one of those cosy British TV children's shows. From Moreton-in-Marsh, we bus it through the same type of scenery to Chipping Campden. Both these villages sit within the Cotswolds' Area of Outstanding Natural Beauty (AONB), the largest in Great Britain and many claim the most stunning. It's an impression helped by the fact that the Cotswold region is 80% farmland, interspersed with magical woodlands, myriad wild animals and birds and some of the most picturesque villages you will find.

Chipping Campden, also happens to be the starting point for the Cotswold Way national trail, a walk that we are determined to see through to the end. Although we think of ourselves as relatively fit, the walk *does* promise to be a challenge, taking us from Chipping Campden at the northern end of the Cotswolds, to the Roman city of Bath in the south. The trail covers a distance of 102 miles, or 160 kilometres, often doubling back, becoming at times almost circular, scaling every available hill and ensuring that the longest possible route is taken between each village. But it also has a reputation for taking you through some of the most glorious country in all the UK. Winding through deep, lush green woods, across open fields, past medieval churches, Roman ruins and ancient long barrows, it regularly diverts into little known but beautiful villages that dot the entire route. It sounds divine.

And that is why we've decided to take a full two weeks for the walk. Many who attempt this walk do it in sections of three or four days at a time over several sessions. For those who walk the trail in one go, the average time taken is eight days. Some do it in less, others take longer. When we planned the walk, we were both reluctant to rush from one village to the next, testing our fitness against others. We weren't doing the walk for our physical wellbeing. Nor were we doing it because of some mid-life crisis in which we try to be young and virile again. Rather, the idea was to make sure we participated in our surroundings, taking time to absorb the unique history, culture and beauty we were passing through. And, we wanted to interact with the people who populate these villages, to experience just a little of the life they do.

# Feeling the love in Chipping Campden

The school bus on which we've hitched, winds its way through narrow, shaded roads with overhanging elms and willows for approximately eight miles before dropping us in the High Street of Chipping Campden. It's a street which dates back to the 7th century and still shows signs of ruts left by the medieval carts that creaked along its cobbles. In the Domesday Book of 1086, Chipping Campden's population was recorded as 300 souls and seventy-three households. Its value to the Lord of the Manor (Earl Harold) was annualised at £20. The village also sported twelve slaves, (three of whom were female), twenty-one plough teams, and two mills. To be honest, it looks like little has changed since then, except perhaps, the slaves and the land value. The village has that untouched feel to it that eludes most country settlements. Locals still go about their business in an unhurried way, gossiping with each other in the street, attending village meetings, and organising social days for the church. I suspect they work and play in much the same way as they might have five hundred years ago. There is the medieval market square, late-Saxon churches, dry-stone walls, and traditional honey-coloured Cotswold cottages just as they have always been.

In between, there is a tiny co-op, a hairdressers, several time-honoured speciality shops and numerous historic pubs.

Surrounding the village, which sits in a broad, shallow valley, are the greenest of fields, acres and acres of them populated with flocks of fat, woolly sheep grazing in small packs. They seem oblivious to the lucky straw they drew in being born and bred in such bountiful country, grazing endlessly on pasture that our poor sheep back home in Australia could only dream about. Strolling through narrow lanes, with views over a luxurious, unblemished landscape, it feels as if we have just stepped into a medieval fairy-tale, but without the disease and pestilence that usually plagues its people.

Chipping Campden is an affluent settlement, built almost entirely of stone, dominated by Saxon churches and obviously at peace with itself. Its history has, for many hundreds of years, revolved around the lucrative wool trade and taking one look at these sheep, you get an idea of just how lucrative it must have been. The affluence has continued. It still has its fat sheep and inherited wealth, but also the retired, rich and part-time residents from London's financial district.

The village's historic character also attracts the usual gaggle of celebrities, attempting to escape their place in the spotlight for a moment's peace somewhere secluded but civilised. Their idea of *getting back to basics*, after all, is a place with access to all their needs and wants and only a short jog from the city. When filming The Libertine, that famous and more famously troubled Hollywood star – Johnny Depp – decided Chipping Campden was his favourite place to be. He would often be seen walking the town, making himself at home in one of the local pubs, or simply seeking some Cotswold solitude. The equally brilliant though somewhat less celebrated cellist -Julian Lloyd Webber - went so far as to make his home here, becoming a regular in Chipping Campden's annual music festival. Eventually, though, even he couldn't ignore the limelight altogether, and moved back to the big city.

Despite these periodic brushes with fame, the village has a delightfully authentic feel to it, blessedly devoid of the 'touristic' fabric that weaves its way through some of the other chocolate-box villages. Our own accommodation for the next couple of nights is the King's Hotel – the largest of its kind in town and in beautiful condition despite its great age. The room we have is large and tastefully decorated and its view captures the small, dreamlike beauty of this village. It's a tranquil scene. There are, perhaps, half a dozen people strolling though town, no more. We watch a woman emerge from the co-op and call goodbye to the shopkeeper, before crossing the road to her own house. Another enters the hairdresser's in the middle of the square. A brewery truck is delivering new kegs to the back of our hotel while the pub across the road is opening its doors for the first trade of the day. It's a village with its own purpose, doing what it's been doing for hundreds of years.

The afternoon is all ours so it's downstairs and out the door after a quick call to the baggage transfer company. We have arranged with one of the local transfer companies to pick up our heavier bags each morning and deliver them to the next stop on the trail. For a very reasonable fee of £9 per bag per day we figure this is by far the best way to go. All we'll take each day is our day pack with lunch, water and rain gear.

Within 200 feet from the hotel we pass no less than three pubs, all open, all with punters. There are actually ten pubs in this village. Trying to acclimatise ourselves, a swift turn is taken to the right, through a stone archway and straight through the door of the Lygon Arms. The plaque on the inside wall claims the pub is approximately four hundred and fifty-years old, an age confirmed by the low ceilings, bowed wooden benches, and crooked, thick stone walls. Originally, it was a coaching inn and still has its narrow cobbled "driveway" and low arch, through which the coaches passed. Horses were taken to the rear of the inn to feed, while their drivers ate and drank their fill inside. It's picture perfect.

Fronting up to the bar I take in the bewildering selection of beers on tap. None of them mean anything to me, but being a typical Australian, obsessed with ice-cold beer, I ask the landlady which of the offerings are chilled. She looks at me as if I might be a little slow and says; "well they all are love".

"Right, but which might be *really* cold".

"They are all *really* cold" she says a little more sternly, "they come straight from the cellar".

"Ah, so not refrigerated?"

"Well the cellar is cold".

I apologise for being so precious and ask for two bottles of Peroni from the fridge. She gives an audible sigh and bends to get them.

Apart from this somewhat tense introduction, Wendy and I spend the next couple of hours settling into the pub's atmosphere and getting on famously with the landlady. She fills us in on the pub's history, the best places to eat (including her pub) and places to steer clear of. Three of the locals wander over to join in the chat, ask us the usual questions and relay a few of their own stories. The interaction is easy and relaxed and we both feel quite at home in this charming, 16th century relic.

Chipping Campden, like much of the Cotswolds, is a place of extraordinary events over thousands of years. On Dover's Hill, at the top of the village, is the Kiftsgate Stone, which marks a meeting place of Celtic tribes who gathered here around three thousand years ago to pay homage to their gods, swap wives and trade sought after goods. Later, Romans passed through the village on their regular trade routes. Centuries after its first inhabitants, Dover's Hill became the site of the Cotswold's 'Olimpik Games', which began their life as early as 1612. They mainly involved running down the hill faster than the next bloke. Much more recently, the village was home to William Morris, as well as the famously left-wing author Graham Greene. He wrote of class wars and poverty at the hands of capitalists while luxuriating in his beautiful Cotswold house in England's most affluent region.

After an afternoon taking in the sights, it is almost dinner time, and the pub beckons once again. By now, the atmosphere inside has changed dramatically. It is standing room only, three or four-deep at the bar, every seat taken, except fortunately, the ones we've reserved. I think that just about every resident of the village must be in here. A few have even brought their dogs. The mood is merry, people talking, laughing, joking with each other. We sit down and join the fun, lubricating ourselves with a couple of (chilled) ales, before beginning on a monstrous pub meal that consumes our attentions for the next half an hour.

The air is close and warm with so many bodies pressing up against each other, but right now we could not think of a better place to be. The Lygon Arms is the type of pub you want to make your local, the type which would see you turning up of an afternoon for a couple of 'swift halves' and then Friday nights for your regular pub meal and social get-together. It's a place where

I think you might develop lasting friendships and become part of a small, close community. I just wish we had one like it at home.

## Ready, set.....walk

Our final morning in Chipping Campden marks the beginning of our longed-for adventure. Bags are being picked up at 9.am for delivery to the B&B in Broadway, so it's day packs on and that's really all we have to worry about. First, photos are taken next to the small stone obelisk outside the medieval Market Hall. This marks the walk's starting point, with a reminder that it's exactly 102 miles to Bath. A perfect morning greets us – cool breeze, clear blue sky and a chorus of Spring birdsong. Our moods are high. Adventure is in the air and excitement is in our bones.

The Cotswold Way is one of Britain's great national trails. Much of the route can be traced back at least six thousand years to the early Neolithic age and is littered with archaeological remnants from that period. In fact, a rich and rewarding history accompanies this trail for its entire length, and I'm keen as mustard to explore. Today, Wendy and I are creating our own little bit of history. As insignificant as we are, we're also participants in this ancient path. And it is indeed a humbling experience to know you will be walking a trail that your ancestors have walked for thousands of years, on their own errands, facing their own pressures and opportunities, fears and triumphs. In a way, we all touch their world, as they do ours. We share their DNA after all, carrying their countless lives through our own existence. But right here, right now, we can simply try to imagine life in the mists of prehistory, when gods, not science, determined people's future.

Hopefully, today we'll be having a relatively easy time of it, with a walk of just under 10 kilometres or about 6 miles to the larger village of Broadway. I think this leg is meant to ease you into the trail so you're not immediately scared off by the climbs and distances that still await you further on. Up the long, breathless Dover's Hill and onto a wide, grassy ridge, the scenery is matching the weather, providing the most glorious views to the village below. Near the top of the climb, a couple is approaching us from a small side track. Amazingly, they're already lost. Holding their map up to us, they ask if we're doing the Cotswold Trail and if so, where it might be. At this stage the trail is still clearly marked so we politely point out its line ahead, but decide *not* to become their walking companions. At the risk of sounding hermit-like, this is *our* time and we want to do it *our* way.

I actually thought there would be many more people on the trail. There are no more than four couples within sight and we've been told that the first day is always the most crowded. Soon, we come to the first of what I later learn is a "kissing gate". These ingenious little contraptions have no lock but are weighted in such a way that they stay closed until a lever is lifted. Even as you walk through them, the field on either side remains closed-off so that animals have no hope of escape. After you have passed through, both sides of the gate swing back to touch each other gently, hence the name "kissing". This initial gate turns out to be the first of hundreds we encounter along the trail, each with a sign reminding walkers to be responsible when crossing private land.

One of the most exceptional qualities of UK walking trails is their absolute right of way at all times. It's a right that has been fought for long and hard and is protected with a fierce determination. Across England and Wales, it is now also an enforceable right by law. A trail such as the Cotswold Way cuts across both public and private land (usually farms) and the private landholders are obliged to keep the track open, clear of obstructions and properly marked through their property. This means you have the luxury of walking through beautiful, unspoilt landscapes for the entire journey. It's not just the national trails either. There are walking tracks criss-crossing each other right across the country, providing the walking public with a variety of adventures, and people like us with much confusion.

According to Dr. Mike Christie, there are more than 117,000 miles of public rights of way, with another one million hectares becoming available after the Countryside and Rights of Way Act. That's a heck of lot of available walking route for the average Joe to ramble across. It means that you and I can access just about any part of this Island that we wish, wandering to our heart's content. We could walk for years without seeing the same thing twice.

And the English really do make use of this great privilege, usually with their trusty dogs. Christie claims that these lucky people clock up more than 527 million walking trips each year. That works out to almost ten such trips per person. What's more, it also seems helpful to the economy. Christie estimates that annual expenditure by Brits on this single activity is between £1.4 billion and £2.7 billion, as well as supporting up to 245,000 full-time jobs. Walking is not only healthy, but profitable. The more these guys walk, the better their economy ticks over. Perhaps they could call for a national walking campaign if and when the next GFC raises its head.

We could also take some lessons back home, where you'd be lucky to get one in a hundred people doing such a trip. The great irony for us in Australia is that it's one of the largest countries on the planet and yet almost completely closed off to walkers through lack of public pathways. Unless you confine yourself to national parks, most walking in Australia has to be undertaken on the side of roads, where you battle a constant stream of cars and worse, trucks. Not the most relaxing or enjoyable of options. Fields, farms and crown land are securely fenced off to the public, providing an effective barrier between the people and their land. The vast majority of our country remains off-limits and invisible to its inhabitants. Whereas here in the tiny island of Britain, a nation a fraction the size of our own, you have the freedom of open spaces and an opportunity to discover the country in full. You can simply pick a direction and walk, always finding a suitable trail to take you. Space doesn't always correlate with freedom. The lesson is, open up the country, create walking paths and people will walk...maybe.

The trail is still treating us kindly, a few gentle hills followed by ridgeways and shallow valleys. Wendy and I take our time, chatting to fellow walkers as we cross paths, taking in the endlessly picturesque scenery, and snapping far too many photos. I've brought my new Nikon DSLR with me for this trip and the novelty hasn't quite worn off. I take photos of anything and everything that moves. Fortunately, I learnt early on that taking the lazy option and switching the camera to "fully automatic" mode allows it to take much better photos than I ever could on "manual". So, for this walk "automatic" is where it stays. It's a sad but true reflection of my photography skills. Nevertheless, optimism is the flavour of this day as weather, landscape and gentle paths combine to lull us into a false sense of comfort. Unwisely, we begin to think that the whole walk might be a doddle.

We have already experienced several more "kissing gates", attracted a small, dancing flock of wood warblers and piqued the interest of some exceedingly well-fed dairy cows. I am thinking to myself that right now, the world and its troubles seem a distant and fading memory. There is so much pleasure to take from our surroundings, the solitude, the beauty, that I just smile to myself and enjoy.

In the medium distance a tall, grey, stone structure in the form of a narrow castle interrupts our view. Our guidebook tells us this is Broadway Tower, apparently the thought-bubble of Capability Brown and James Wyatt in the late 1700s. Designed as a "Saxon Tower", it has since been referred to as one of Brown's Follies. It serves no real purpose other than to surprise walkers as they come up over the hill. Nevertheless, it's quite a stunning monument, fooling many into thinking it some early medieval military structure. From its base you can catch the most panoramic views across the entire Cotswold region, over to Tewksbury and Bredon Hill in the east, all the way to Gloucester and even Cirencester in the north. It entices us into taking another dozen photos from every angle. The joy, or *folly*, of a digital camera. From here, it's a downhill run (or slow walk) into the village of Broadway. It's not until now that we realise how much of the walk has been uphill, because the decline is long and not too gentle. But at this stage of the day, much better to be going down than up.

## Broadway elegance

Arriving in Broadway at a much earlier than anticipated 1.pm, there's still another two hours until we can check into our B&B. There's nothing for it but to head into the very attractive grey-stone pub – *The Horse and Hound* - for a swift half. Wendy and I discover early on that walking the Cotswold Way is thirsty work. Fortunately, one of the great delights of this trail is the abundance of local public houses that so kindly and conveniently come to your rescue. After resting in the luxury of a couple of deep, leather armchairs, sipping a local bitter or two and chomping through several bags of crisps, it's time to take a proper look around the village.

Broadway is an elegant Cotswold village, with its honey-coloured stone cottages, here more substantial than most, its numerous pubs, perfectly manicured hedges and lawns and village greens, expensively restored dry-stone walls and an undeniable air of affluence. It is a larger and busier village than Chipping Campden, with around 2,500 residents, but retains every bit of the Cotswold charm. Broadway also shares a history littered with distinct markers of human civilisation. The village dates back more than five thousand years and was once home to a thriving settlement of Beaker People. Later, it hosted the Mercian Kings, that most powerful clan of Britain's early Saxon history. They, in fact, left a legacy of characteristics, language and looks that many of us possess today. Even later still, Broadway became one of the major drivers in England's innovative Arts and Craft Movement. From this region, the movement spread throughout the rest of Europe and North America and by the late 1800s, had changed the fundamentals of design and decoration across the developed world.

Today, with its well-cared for properties and wide, tree-lined streets, Broadway looks more like first prize in a postcard competition. Crossing the road, we have to jump to the kerb in order to avoid a sleek, yellow convertible Bentley that is gliding slowly to a stop. The gent driving looks to be in his sixties while his young blond wife looks about half that age. She is being deposited for what I assume is her weekly hairdressing appointment. Other, beautifully dressed women also make their way to the same door with their morning make-up so meticulously applied. You get the impression that this is how a lot of Cotswold folk spend their time, strolling from one pampering session to another, pottering in their manicured gardens, and chatting about the dramatic rise in their property values. Perhaps I am over-generalising. In fact, I'm almost certain I am. Our visit to a smaller Broadway pub this evening will show us another, earthier side to the village.

Having secured our lodgings for the night in what appears to be one of Broadway's more luxurious residences, Wendy and I set off in a chipper mood to perhaps try another *not so swift* half and find a place for dinner. We are both ravenous from the walk. There doesn't appear to be a lot of culinary variety in Broadway. You have a choice of a pub meal in one of the traditional Broadway hotels, or a pub meal in one of the cafes and family restaurants. We settle for a pub meal in the *Crown and Trumpet.* Unlike the *Horse and Hound*, which obviously caters to tourists and the trendier set, this pub oozes authenticity. It is a local watering hole at the other end of town and tonight, at least, is populated exclusively by locals.

The small, low ceilinged pub is packed and as Wendy and I swing open the door, the entire room of patrons turns to stare. Most give us a welcoming smile, so we march on in. After ten minutes of waiting a table is free, so Wendy grabs it while I head to the bar. Immediately, I do a double-take. There's a young, fair-haired fellow with a large bushy beard standing at the bar in his work clothes, and next to him is standing his large Irish Setter dog. I don't mean the dog is just next to him, I mean he's actually standing on his two hind legs with his front paws up on the bar. I walk up and take my place next to them. The fellow turns and smiles and his dog wags its tail. I smile back and think, "can't get earthier than this".

We dine on a hearty meal of beef stew and maybe a couple too many pints. But the place is wonderful, and we're beginning to really appreciate the endearing pub culture of the English. It gives us a tiny glimpse into the ties that bind these communities so closely together. I imagine many of the locals see their pub as much more than a watering hole. For them, it seems a place of friendship, of security, a place that safeguards their village's position in the world. It can be difficult for an outsider to understand this. Yes, we have pubs and they have their regulars, but our pubs are not representative of a particular village or town, of a way of life that is different to the village next door. They do not provide the sanctuary of idiosyncratic camaraderie and shared understandings that these village pubs represent. I just love the uniqueness of these ancient watering holes.

*Back on the trail*

The second morning of our walk is pretty well a clone of the first. The sun is shining brightly in an azure sky with only the lightest of breezes. Even the weather seems to be imitating the charmed beauty of this area. Today, we're heading for a village by the name of Toddington, not one of the usual overnight villages on the trail, but the only one in which we could find accommodation. The second day's hike is another shortish one of around 12kms, or 7.5 miles. But the distance masks the many hills, some steep, that stand in our way. The route out of Broadway is through the most glorious, green fields, punctuated by large English Oak, Elm and Beech trees. They cast large areas of shade under which dairy cows gather and munch happily. It is an enchanting start to the day. We have worked our way through a substantial English breakfast, there aren't too many aches or pains from yesterday's efforts, our walking shoes are wearing in nicely, and spirits are high. This is walking at its best. Passing Snowshill Road on our right and later, the Wychaven Way on our left it is a walker's dream here. You're always surrounded by uncluttered landscapes and an assortment of animals. What a wonderland to have right on your doorstep!

## Everyone's lost

Wendy, who has been reading our Cotswold guide book assiduously, suggests we take an easy diversion through the historic hamlet of Snowshill. I'm reluctant, as this new way bypasses the historic Burhill Fort. Plus, I always seem to come out of *diversions* far less happy than when I go in. Apart from getting lost, which is almost inevitable, the place to which I am *diverting*, is usually a disappointment. Wendy convinces me, however, that Snowshill is definitely worth the diversion and the path is clearly marked all the way, but for some reason, not the obvious *Snowshill Way* we have just passed. Early on in our relationship, I learnt that when my wife makes up her mind to do something, it is more than a little foolish to argue. A steely look sets in her eyes, her mouth tightens and you just know it's time to shut-up. So off to Snowshill we go.

After half a mile or so, the Cotswold Way signs evaporate. We discover, over the remainder of our walk, that these signs proliferate when there is only one trail to follow, and have a habit of disappearing when things become a bit confusing. Our guidebook, on which we are now relying, advises us to "take the track beside the fence, heading down the hill". Well let me tell you, at the moment there are four *different* tracks intersecting and at least two of them follow a fence, and these two are leading off in completely different directions. I turn an accusing eye on Wendy, who studiously ignores me, and immerses herself in the guidebook. "OK", she announces, pointing ahead "it has to be this track here". I try to share her confidence and follow obediently behind. Before too long we come to another intersection of paths, again with no signage and our book is no clearer, advising us to "take the path through attractively undulating grassland". What the heck does that mean? It is *all* "attractively undulating grassland".

By now, Wendy is looking a little less certain. Actually, she looks lost. I am ranting about dubious directions and she is ranting about it not being her fault, so we decide to rant together about incompetent trail markers and books that pretend to be helpful. Mark this down as another minus for *diversions*. As we both search for some hidden clue, there is an exasperated "hello" from our left. A middle-aged woman is climbing over a barbed-wire fence, looking tired, sweaty, and thoroughly fed-up. She approaches, smiling weakly and immediately asks "Do you have any idea where we are?" Funny, I was going to ask *her* that.

Wendy giggles sheepishly and tells her that we are also kind of lost. The woman, who we learn is Linda from Melbourne, Australia, pulls out a large map. It's even more incomprehensible than our book. "I've been walking around in circles for more than two hours" she almost cries. "I'm trying to get to Broadway". "Ah, we've just come from there", and we try to give our best directions. She's happy, but we're no wiser.

## Serenading in Snowshill

As it turns out, Snowshill is, without doubt, worth the *diversion*. It's a tiny hamlet nestled into the side of a hill. There is one, very narrow main street lined with pocket-sized cottages that don't seem to have a straight wall between them. They are all semi-detached and huddle together in quite an amusingly crooked fashion. The cottages are of the traditional Cotswold stone, with grey, shingle roofs and strangely, every one with a bright blue door. Each is almost identical to the next and that's probably because they were once tenanted to the domestic workers of Snowshill Manor. The Lord of the Manor, who, from the 820s, also happened to be the Bishop of Winchcombe Abbey, built them for the workers. Being a good Catholic, he saved money on floor space. Because when I say *pocket-sized*, I mean it.

Opposite these cottages, on the other side of the single main road is the lonely and somewhat eerie looking Snowshill pub, imaginatively named the *Snowshill Arms*. It too is tiny, fitting approximately a dozen people at a squeeze and dates back to the 13th century. When you consider that the current population of Snowshill stands at a mere 164 people, one street of cottages and one small pub is plenty. The entire hamlet was centred on and revolved around the Manor House and its variously eccentric occupants. But the history of this little blip in the landscape is a long one, reaching back to about 4000 BC. The Manor House, which now attracts thousands of tourists each year, was last owned by Charles Paget Wade. He was an architect who took eccentricity to new levels by filling the Manor House so full with his strange and wonderful collections that he couldn't fit in himself. Instead, he had to live in one of the small garden cottages on the perimeter of the estate. The villagers claim this cottage remains haunted, by not one, but two ghosts. The first is an old monk who lived here for a time in the estate's early years, and the second, a young woman who was forced to marry against her will in an upstairs bedroom, probably to the old monk.

Turning back into the street, Wendy and I stare in through the pub's small, dusty windows to see three people inside, who in turn stare at us. It's still too early for lunch so we head back across the road to take up camp on the only village green, which is about six feet by six feet. We demolish a morning tea of fruit and cheese and the ubiquitous English oat cakes that we packed last night. One quick glance up and down the road allows you to take in the entire village. The road slopes gradually downhill to a winding stream murmuring away happily, with majestic English Elm and Willow trees lining its banks. Across the bridge and beyond are fields of vibrant lavender, its deep mauve contrasting stunningly with the green of surrounding fields. Snowshill is the type of place you could relax into for an entire day, doing nothing but absorbing the tranquillity, sunshine and soft birdsong that transport you into a quieter world. I think you could search the whole of England and not find a cuter, and perhaps stranger village. But enough dreaming. Time to pack up and make our way to tonight's resting place.

*Undercover*

Our guidebook tells us that next, we'll come across the village of Stanton. But before anything can be read about it, Wendy announces that it's once again time for a toilet stop. I give an inward groan but smile and offer to mind her backpack while she trots off to find one of her special bushes. This is number four in the last three hours and I know there'll be several more before we reach Toddington. The toilet stop is fine, but my wife is not the most decisive person you will ever meet so it usually takes her a good few minutes to select a spot with all the right attributes. All in all, I plan on ten minutes for each stop. When you calculate that not a day passes without six or seven of these, you are forced to add more than an hour to your walking plan. She insists that I go 'look-out' each time and as you can imagine I get a little bored standing around until she finishes. This time for a bit of fun, I wait until she's fully occupied before calling out "Oh, hello" to an imaginary on-comer. The result is astounding. Wendy bounces up from behind the bush whilst at the same time attempting to pull up her pants. Her face is white, her eyes popping and of course she trips, falling on her backside in a not too elegant fashion. I collapse in hysterics. It goes without saying that when she realises the bluff, my situation becomes suddenly precarious. She chases me down the track threatening all sorts of retaliation. I figure, in the end, it was worth it.


An aspect of the walk that neither of us had expected, is the constant, melodic birdsong that accompanies us throughout each day. Apparently, most of it is down to these little creatures by the name of *Great Tit* and *Blue Tit* who sing their tiny hearts out. There's also a Coal Tit, but we haven't come across one yet. They have a repertoire of around forty calls and like to amuse themselves by repeating all of them over and over. They are also very territorial, avidly guarding their space and never leaving the spot in which they were born. All in all, Britain has no less than two million pairs of these little critters, so you can get some idea of how constant their companionship is on this walk. Whether out in open fields or walking through forest tracks, these birds dance across our path weaving their magical songs around us and lending an almost mystical quality to the day. Sometimes we just walk quietly, allowing their music to wash over us. It's a wonderful way to spend your time.

The trail now leads in the direction of *Buckland Wood* and I feel we're entering another fairy tale, one that must once have been inhabited by the great JRR Tolkien when writing his tome - The Lord of the Rings. Of course, Tolkien, an Oxford Professor of English, as well as poet and philosopher, spent much of his life roaming through the Cotswolds and obviously picked up some of his unique names and descriptions in this very area. A great deal of the Cotswolds could easily be transported to *Middle Earth* and not seem out of place. Perhaps some of the characters we meet could fit in quite well too. In fact, it is rumoured, (mainly among folk living here) that the unique trees grown in the village of Stow-on-the-Wold were Tolkien's inspiration for the *Doors of Moria* and that the Bell Inn pub in Moreton-in-Marsh, is the basis for his *Prancing Pony* pub.

## Nobody's home

Making our way across more *Shire-like* fields littered with cattle, the ubiquitous Cotswold sheep and seemingly wild horses, it's not long before we are heading down a long hill into the hamlet of Stanton. Unlike the usual mirage when approaching a place, Stanton actually looks smaller the closer you get to it. Finally, when entering the main street, it comes to resemble a toy village designed to a scaled model somewhat less than 1:1. Exaggerating this impression, the entire village also appears empty. It's as if someone built a beautiful village for people to look at but not live in. There are two rows of neat cottages, all built in the honey Cotswold stone that reflects the sun with that eerie glow, all much the same design, all owned by obviously affluent residents but with absolutely no sign of life. There's not a single shop or café, no guesthouses, no post office, just a solitary pub at the top of the hill. Even the *Great Tits* are silent here.

There's the mandatory church and Manor House, with its traditionally large dimensions and enormous chimneys along the roofline. It was built in the mid-sixteenth century, with architecture and decorations, typically Elizabethan. But there are no visitors at either place. Instead, the buildings stand in silent watchfulness over the equally silent village. The population today numbers 198 souls, a dramatic increase on the 20 souls, six of whom were slaves, recorded in the Domesday Book. Although, when you consider it took almost a thousand years to reach these heady heights, perhaps not so astounding after all.

It's lunch time and we're both ravenous. The 17th century pub at the top of the village – The Mount Inn – looks nice although deserted, but it is at the end of a long uphill climb and we are in no mood to take any more steps right now. Instead, we head for a single bench on the tiny village green at the centre of the village. Here, we strip off our walking boots, peel off socks and demolish our inadequate lunches. The sun on our faces is delicious and I lie back on the grass to soak it in. But too soon, I'm rudely prodded out of a pleasant doze and it's up and off again. I think if you're after a glimpse of pure aesthetic beauty then Stanton is a must see, but I suspect you'll be left strangely unfulfilled by the unequivocal void in its heart.

The next half mile of walking is across open fields that just happen to host a herd of fat black and white cows and what looks suspiciously like a bull in their midst. As we draw nearer, the herd *and* bull turn to watch us, and Wendy's pace slows noticeably. She has strategically placed herself behind me while mumbling words of encouragement and something about the bull looking docile anyway. I don't know what *she's* looking at but this bull does *not* look docile. In fact, he's taking a very keen interest in us. Well me, actually, because Wendy has now stopped and left me out in the middle of the paddock by myself. From a safe distance she calls out that she's read some amazing statistic on cow and bull attacks in the UK and that people have actually been killed by them. Thanks for that.


Since I'm already out here on my own I decide to keep walking. I try to steer clear of the herd without looking worried as I'm pretty sure they pick up on any scent of fear. It apparently feeds some perverse and sadistic part of their nature. Looking straight ahead, I walk just a bit quicker than normal. The bull isn't fooled. Wendy calls out, with what sounds ever so slightly like a chuckle in her voice, that I am being followed. By now the bull has broken away from the herd and is closing in on me. My practiced air of nonchalance evaporates and I take off in the direction of a gate too far away. This sudden action has effectively relieved the bull of any boredom he may have been feeling. He decides to give chase. Wendy shrieks at me to run. "What the hell do you think

I'm doing" I call back. And then the adrenaline really kicks in. By the time I reach the gate I pretty well vault it mid-stride, something I still can't believe I managed. The chase is over and typically, the bull takes no interest whatsoever in Wendy, leaving her to walk casually over to the gate, still laughing, still telling me about the danger of attacks in the UK. Suddenly, I need a toilet break.

Heading through more open fields, with large Elms, Horse Chestnuts and Beech trees, and flocks of fat black-faced sheep, we stumble onto a beautifully manicured cricket ground, seemingly in the middle of nowhere. There are the customary changing rooms, the scoreboard, a perfectly kept pitch and not a soul in sight. It is literally in the middle of grazing fields. With these tiny villages, I can't believe there are enough people under seventy to make up a team. But the ground is meticulously maintained, and ready for action. You have to hand it to the Poms, they will put a cricket pitch anywhere in the hopes of generating interest.

Now, the path winds its way between two long, thick hedgerows before crossing a crystal-clear stream. The water must be 99.9%

pure and it's so tempting to squat down and drink our fill. There are too many stories, however, of seemingly pure water that is contaminated with cow and sheep manure, as well as an unwholesome mixture of fertilisers, so we resist. Instead, we cross the rustic, limestone bridge that through time must have helped many thousands cross this stream, and, I imagine, will help thousands more before its days come to an end.

In another mile or so we enter the equally deserted village of Stanway. Records tells us that Stanway has 343 residents hiding away somewhere, so a veritable metropolis compared to Snowshill and Stanton. For now, though, it's just Wendy and me, along with the Jacobean Manor House (Stanway House), which was given away by the rhythmic pair *Odo* and *Dodo*, in 715. Now, the Manor is owned and lived in by the Earl of Wemyss, who occasionally lets the public in to view a whole new level of austerity. From the outside it's an imposing and no doubt once grand Manor House that has simply fallen into disrepair. Each of the fifteen-foot windows looks out cheerily onto the ancient cemetery in which many of the Earl's family are buried. In fact, his family has lived in and around Stanway for the past eight hundred years, as I imagine *many* of the local families here have. It makes you wonder at the level of inbreeding in a place like this. I reckon 343 people are roughly equivalent to 76 families, who have lived in extremely close, isolated contact for the past 800 years, with not a lot to do. Perhaps that's why they all stay firmly indoors.

I wonder if the thick dry-stone walls around the hamlet have had anything to do with it. One of the most common features of this walk so far has been these endless walls. Dry-stone walls are prominent in this part of England as well as at the other end of the country, in the Yorkshire Dales. Skilled masons craft them in meticulous fashion and may spend months on one assignment. It has been described as a trade by some of the more ignorant, but others debate whether it's an art or a craft. I think looking at these walls, you'd be hard pressed not to call it art. They are as beautiful and require as much skill as pretty well anything I can think of. They have also been around a heck of a long time. The first evidence of dry-stone walling in England reaches back five thousand years to, you guessed it, the stone age. Late Neolithic farmers built them aplenty, as a means of keeping their herds contained. A little later, the walls doubled as defences around villages, causing invaders to at least pause for thought before going through with an attack. In the18th century, they came back into fashion as a means of herd containment and later again, in the Great Depression, as a means of deterring desperate neighbours from stealing cattle, sheep, and crops.

Today, dry-stone walls are the fashion of wealthy Cotswold second-homers who migrate from London on weekends. These people tend to like their privacy and social status in equal amounts and are rather taken with the idea of fencing the world off from their properties. They also like to advertise the fact that they can do it in style. The Dry-Stone Walling Association of Great Britain lists only seven non-quarry companies in the whole land, fourteen if you count the quarry miners as well. That's not many. If you do the economics, it's obvious that huge demand divided by very few masons, equals astronomical prices.

It is said that if you joined all the dry-stone walls of the Cotswolds, their length would be longer than China's Great Wall. I think they're right. But these walls are *seriously* well made, beautifully in fact. There is no mortar or binding material, just dry stones carved to a rectangular, flat shape that lock together. They can sit in this state for hundreds of years before needing repair and then good luck finding someone capable of fixing them, or the money to pay for it.

## Talking B&Bs

Wood Stanway, which is largely an extension of Stanway, is little more than an indulgence of its residents. They insisted on differentiating their neck of the woods in an effort to move upmarket. Apparently, the residents here think their neighbourhood's a little better than that of Stanway, even though they don't have the grand Manor House, or perhaps because of it. Anyway, they wanted their own bit of the Cotswolds where they could mingle without interference from the larger namesake next door and to my mind, it *is* a little prettier. Maybe they just didn't want to share their neighbours' *breeding pool*. It's here that we divert and leave the trail for the night. Tonight, we are hosted by a woman who's graciously agreed to open her "part-time" B&B for two desperate travellers. We were unable to find any other accommodation in this area tonight and so appealed to what we hoped was this woman's good nature. Perhaps if we're extra nice she'll extend the grace enough to drop us back to the trail in the morning, because her place turns out to be quite a hike.

Toddington, we are told, is a larger village about two miles down a B Road, which the host warned us was "a bit busy this time of day". She actually offered to pick us up, but my too polite wife assured her it wouldn't be a problem for us to walk. So, walk we do, along the footpath-free side of a narrow road that semi-trailers pretend is a speedway. On the narrowest parts, of which there are many, we have to scramble up a slippery bank each time a truck approaches, just to stay alive. Sharing the roads with these trucks, are manic school mums racing to pick up their *beloveds*. They seem to take delight in seeing how close they can get without actually hitting us. It's certainly not one of our more enjoyable walking experiences. Finally, frustrated, stressed and hating British B Roads, we walk into the thoroughly unimpressive village of Toddington. Perhaps it's simply our mood, but the place seems without character. It sits at the junction of several busy B Roads and lacks the architecture, village atmosphere or heart that we have been experiencing elsewhere. I think it could better be described as a meeting of roads than a village.

But we're only here for the night and the B&B in which we're staying looks large and welcoming. It's also across the road from the village's only pub and the host was thoughtful enough to reserve us a table for dinner. She and her husband are delightful, she, late-forties, reserved and polite, he a gregarious fifty-year-old, hyper-active and obviously craving a chat. Both clearly belong to that upper echelon of British society enjoying a semi-retired lifestyle, with plenty of time and money to spare. They're well educated, entitled and have definite views on how things should be run and, more importantly, who should be running them.

She dabbles in B&B hosting as a hobby and a way of meeting new people, very clearly not for the money. The provisions for our night's 'comfort', include Armani toiletries and Hugo Boss bath towels. Breakfast alone would have consumed every penny of the night's lodging fee. There's a strong possibility she also hosts to gain a reprieve from her husband's constant banter. She *does* seem happy that he's following *us* around and not *her*. He's actually an interesting chap and very informed about his world, but he can *really* talk. For the first hour he follows us from room to room, finding out everything he can about our trip and what we do, and telling us intimate details of his own life story in return. This includes his plans for the night and the music he intends to listen to while his wife's out at a race horse owner's meeting. She shoots us apologetic glances while gently telling him to leave us be. Eventually, we make our excuses and exit to the relative quiet of the pub, with her following us out the door. I fear the poor chap is home alone quite often.

I may well be jumping to conclusions, but it has struck me that since we've been in England, each of the B&B hosts appears to be quite nicely off. I'm sure it's just the area we're in, but none of our hosts seem to need the income, seemingly doing it more for the variety and interest. Their houses are large, beautifully furnished and usually situated in luxurious surroundings. The provisions are overly generous and of a high quality. And their accents, interests and education point to lives of privilege. I had always had a perception of English B&Bs as a bit dowdy, a bit basic and not offering the levels of accommodation you would expect from any reasonable hotel. So far, however, nothing could be further from the truth. Perhaps as we migrate south this will change somewhat.

From what I read, B&Bs in Britain are, in fact, doing rather nicely. In 2011 there was a prediction that the humble B&B, which had been losing market share for the previous few years, would continue its slow decline. But it seems the old B&Bs got smart. Since early 2012 their market share and occupancy rates, now averaging around 79%, have, instead, seen a steady increase. The battle between them and the hotel association continues as each sling off at the inadequacies of the other, but B&Bs did something the hotels could not. They hitched up with the AirBnB phenomenon and began listing themselves both under their own banner, and this new one. They simply translate their advertisements into "single rooms" under AirBnB and cash in on its global popularity.

And the Brits just do B&B so darned well. They have, in fact, been providing bed and breakfast accommodation on a commercial basis since the mid-1700s. In the earliest days these B&Bs also included stables for travellers' horses and were spaced roughly a day's ride from each other between major cities and towns. They were also somewhat less comfortable than we expect today, usually providing the traveller with a straw mattress alongside the host's family, or even in the hall or kitchen if space was short. The widespread introduction of the railroad network through Britain was when the industry really came into its own and began providing accommodation in an organised, professional way. So, I suppose that after nearly four hundred years of doing such things, it's no surprise that the English understand exactly what a weary traveller would like at the end of a long day's walk. As our walk progresses and our weariness grows, we increasingly appreciate their understanding.

# Monument valleys

The next leg is an eventful one. Mr chatty man is kindly driving us back to where we left the trail yesterday, with strange reminiscences of the previous night and a meandering monologue about his life. But finally, we extricate ourselves from the car to take up our walk again. Today, the journey is to Winchcombe. It's another fine, cool day with very un-English clear skies and sunshine. The walk is only going to cover about six to seven miles, but apparently is filled with numerous distractions and some major climbs, so we pick up the pace while we can. As usual, we begin the day with a long climb. Each night it is a long downhill trek into the village, which ensures the opposite next morning, and this one is certainly getting its money's worth. After a good 25-minute climb, the bench at the top of the plateau beckons, so we take a break, grab our water bottles and sit to admire the exquisite view. I'm pretty sure we can see the entire Cotswolds from this seat, and the view unfolding before us looks like it's taken straight from a Turner or Constable painting. I could sit here in contemplation for quite some time, particularly as that final beer from last night kicks in with a slightly throbbing head, but Wendy is keen to push on.

The trail is now lined with rows of enormous Beech trees that obscure the stone walls beneath. A sign tells us that it has become a bridleway, where walkers and horse-riders share the path. This shared right-of-way is much more than theory. We have been surprised at the number of riders we've met, almost daily on this section of the walk. And why not? It's an idyllic environment for both horse and rider, relatively undisturbed, no traffic, miles of well-trodden paths, stunning views along the way and plenty of open spaces where horses can be given a real work-out.

The first "distraction" is one of many we will come across, the remains of an Iron-Age fort. In the UK you can spend your entire day walking through history. You could set out in any direction any day of the week and you'd be guaranteed to come across the ancient remains of something. You even become a bit snooty about the whole archaeology thing, turning your nose up if it's not quite *ancient* enough. You get excited by Saxon remains, do a bit of a jig when you come across Celtic or Roman remains, and become positively ecstatic when you wander into a Neolithic burial site. If you chance to come across a rare Mesolithic microlith you're looking back as far as 8000 or 9000 BC, which is truly astounding. So, when you encounter a run-of-the-mill 18<sup>th</sup> century artefact, it's really not worth breaking your stride.

This landscape covers and hides multiple worlds beneath, one overlaying the next, from pretty well every age of human civilisation. Each year, when farmers plough their fields, new relics are uncovered to add to the wealth of archaeological treasure that is Britain. And the fact that you can casually come across these remains on a walking trip is, to me, remarkable. I suppose it reinforces the fact that our presence, right here, right now, is nothing more than a Nano-blink in our collective history and that individually, we really are quite insignificant. I know our children's generation would view such a statement as blasphemy. They will tell you they are the most important beings they have ever encountered, but actually, history tends to disagree.

This fort, known as Beckbury Camp, dates to around 2,000 BC. Now these people might not have had the technology and modern conveniences that we enjoy today, but they certainly knew how to defend themselves. Taking advantage of this particularly high hill, the fort provides visibility for up to seventy miles on a clear day. Not only could they see their enemies approaching from some considerable distance, but once they arrived, they would have to work their way through an extremely narrow rampart with a hill on each side from which the defenders could rain down all sorts of missiles.

The design of these forts was so effective and the defence so successful, that they sprang up all over the British Isles, allowing our ancestors to build permanent dwellings and begin some serious farming. In fact, three thousand years later the Saxons reused many of these forts simply because they couldn't come up with a better design themselves. All-in-all, there were approximately three and a half thousand such hill-forts across Britain. These, with the stationary settlements they protected and their wholly new idea of farming, represented the beginning of modern civilisation. When humans stopped roaming, they had time to stop and think and plan and innovate. It created a society that laid the path for how we live today.

Our path right now, though, is leading downhill and into a deeply wooded area where again it cuts through a carpet of wildflowers, bluebells, a sprinkling of daffodils and the white flowers of wild garlic. The kaleidoscope of colours continues to enchant, contrasting with the large Elms and Plane trees that lean over us and shade our path. But just as we are being seduced by this natural cocoon the trees part and we are out in broad daylight as the trail opens into broad grassland. The ground is flat and dry, is bordered on one side by another small woodland and on the other, by what looks like a well-tended orchard. From what we can discover it looks like it might be the Hayles Fruit Farm, which, more than 130 years ago was planted under instruction of Lord Sudely and now grows all sorts of fruit from apples and pears to strawberries, raspberries, gooseberries, and Cobb nuts, whatever they might be.

Up ahead, is another, slightly younger relic by the name of Beckbury Monument. This is a singular standing stone that commemorates the spot where the patriotic, if somewhat destructive Thomas Cromwell, stood to watch his men take apart and demolish Haile's Abbey. The magnificent Abbey, which had stood in splendour for almost three hundred years was torn down in a fit of manic barbarianism in 1539. Today, the forlorn remains stand in splendid isolation. They sit in the centre of a circular lawn, slightly overgrown and the many arches, still beautiful, show severe weathering. Their stones are discoloured and grass grows among their walls and rooftops, but they still hold a majesty, a reverence that demands respect and thoughtfulness.

The destruction was part of King Henry's vehement opposition to the Catholic Church for not granting him a divorce. Cromwell, who had turned sycophancy into a fine art, took Henry's "reform of the church" to extremes by wilfully laying waste to any symbol of that institution he came across. Whether you are in favour of Henry's "reforms" or not, the sad truth is that we lost some very beautiful and historically important artefacts during his royal tantrums. It's a sombre experience to stand here, looking down on the remains of such wanton ruination.

### Loaded distractions

The next hint of violence escalates dramatically as we work our way up the second hill. There is a volley of gunfire, then silence, then more gunfire and we become just a tad anxious about what we'll encounter. With a half-hearted attempt at bravery, however, we try to find the source of such murderous commotion, albeit tentatively and in a semi-crawl. Cresting the hill, the scene opens onto a group of elderly men and women standing in a line and pointing their equally old shotguns into the air. Two fellows crouch behind them feeding discs into a mechanical slingshot. Shooting clay pigeons is of course a national sport and right here in the Cotswolds it's at its zenith. These folk obviously love it. There are the mandatory Range Rovers and Jaguars parked carefully to the side, the berets, cashmere pullovers, and pearls. And they are firing with abandon.

As Wendy and I approach, the fellow in charge calls a halt to their fun and all turn to give us the once over. With immense relief at the not-so-murderous activity in front of us we call out a cheery hello and wander on up to the group. Unlike the stereotypical impression you would normally associate with such a group, they are friendly and relaxed and ready to talk. There are jokes about their somewhat mixed prowess and they even offer to let us "have a go". We decline politely, but the fellow in charge encourages us to stay for a bit and watch them go through their paces. I'd probably rather watch grass grow but we agree and attempt to look enthralled as the mechanical slingshot starts up again. Throughout the next ten minutes of gunfire, smoke, and loud expletives, the leader of the pack chats amiably away to us about his group and their little foibles, with the odd whispered character assassination thrown in.

*Stereotypes*

Another myth exploded. Numerous people, including my own parents who visited the UK every year for some time had warned that "the English are a reserved lot" who take some getting to know. "Don't be put off by their stern character," we were told. Well, I'm here to say that there's been no *reservation*, and no *sternness*. But there *has* been a real generosity of friendship and hospitality. Local walkers on the track, punters in pubs, even shoppers in supermarkets engage us in conversation and willingly give tips on the best places to visit. They *want* to talk, to know where we're from and what our trip involves and will even invite us to join them at their tables. They are *interested* and about as unlike our preconceived notions as you can get.

Interestingly, a recent survey conducted among foreigners living in Britain found that 69% really like living here, the only drawbacks being the *weather* and the *food*. They found the locals to be *exceptionally friendly*. I think it's pretty spot on in each category. I couldn't fault the people in terms of their attitude towards us. I get the whole weather issue. You only have to look at climate charts to see that Britain has a lot of rain and not a lot of sun. In fact, Scotland is the second cloudiest country on the planet. It just so happens that the whole time we are here, the weather is perfect, so I personally have no problems on that front.

As for the reputation of British food, well, there's not a lot you can say in defence of their food. Yes, over the past two decades it *has* improved. But honestly, not a great deal. There *is* a heck of a lot more in the way of Gastro pubs serving a greater repertoire of dishes than the traditional English pub once offered up. Although the variety is greater, however, many of these pubs struggle to live up to their name. Most we come across serve pretty average food. I think the English got a bit carried away with the gastro label. These days any publican who wants to have a crack at offering food with their beer simply puts "Gastro" above the doorway, whether there's a trained chef in residence or not. Usually not. The famous "curry houses" we front up to are also a bit of a disappointment. The dishes tend to be relatively tasteless with little or no hint of chilli to be found. I read that 50% of Britain's curry houses are expected to close over the next decade. I can understand this. The English *do* serve up a great pie and chips with mushy peas, but let's face it, a month or so on this particular delicacy puts you squarely in the frame for a coronary. So, all-in-all, I think it best that we just focus on how *friendly the English are.*

## Spring delights

Crossing some open fields with deep, luxurious grass and more fat Cotswold sheep gorging themselves, extensive woodlands loom before us. It's actually more like a small forest. After another "kissing gate" the track becomes clearly cut, almost like a tunnel, through large, overhanging Elm and Beech trees and sunlight filters through loose canopies. This dense oasis is said to host numerous wild deer, but today, there's no sign of the creatures. There are instead, the odd squirrel and the ubiquitous Wrens, Twitchers and Wood Starlings.

As the trail leads you from one storybook scene to another, the romance of our walk becomes even more endearing. This Cotswold adventure is simply a delight. The woodland floor is a mass of the most fragile, delicate bluebells interspersed with wild garlic. The white flowering garlic running through the forest creates a brilliant carpet display of vibrant colour as far as the eye can see. The smell of it is intoxicating, not overpowering and unpleasant but a wonderfully fresh aroma that awakens senses and taps your spirit. This, together with the ever-present intoxication of damp undergrowth, the perfume of woodland holly, yew and wild orchids and the smoky scent of the great Elms leaves you almost reeling from the onslaught of scents. I could stay in here all day just watching and listening and *living*. Wendy is busy taking photos to add to future memories. We look at each other and smile. We are both in that same, sensual state of happiness.

Alas, it is time to end our reverie and move on. We must make tracks to Winchcombe before failing light leaves us wandering through unknown streets, looking for unfamiliar lodgings. The bridleway that we're following soon becomes *The Pilgrim's Way,* which was walked regularly by Cistercian Monks on pilgrimages to Hailes Abbey. Here, they spent extended periods of time worshipping in solitude, reconnecting with their God and most importantly for the Church, leaving a substantial donation on their way out. But *our* pilgrimage leads in the opposite direction and our place of worship more likely one of the local pubs. Another couple on horseback approach and stop to chat. They live locally and use the bridleway for their daily ride, and what a place to do it. Through gorgeous woodland away from the bustle of life and surrounded by all the delights that nature can offer. I suppose everyone finds their own gods in their own way.

# From mediocre to sublime

I'm not sure what it is about Winchcombe that doesn't appeal. It has a kind of dreariness to it, a greyness that smothers my mood. This is, after all, a village that others have told us is endearing and quaint. But we just don't see it. A number of the shops and cafes have been closed down, adding to a mood of despair, of tiredness that surrounds us. Perhaps it's that we've just had a long walk and are ready to stop, or that directions to our lodgings seem to be taking us to the less savory part of town. Our road is deserted and the gardens unkempt. The houses too, seem somehow sad and neglected.

Our "room" is just that. There is no check-in, just a key-box with combination for entry. Inside it is clean but bare and uninviting. Perversely, this lodging was one of the more expensive of the walk but without doubt, the least appealing. There is a bed, TV, fridge, bathroom and that's it. The walls are bare, the floor is a hardwearing beige carpet and there is a window that looks out onto the carpark. We shower quickly and head out for a dinner that hopefully is a bit more uplifting than our accommodation.

The name "Winchcombe" means "valley with a bend" and the streets have certainly kept to this theme. It is very difficult to walk from one place to another in a straight line. Rather, you are forced to take circuitous routes that wiggle their way around and through and over before delivering you to the spot that you could actually see just two-hundred yards along the road. The town, of around 4,500 souls is a medieval Saxon settlement, although to look at it you would be hard put to place it in *any* time period. There is a mixture of modern Cotswold stone 'new-build' interspersed with dilapidated medieval structures that appear to have been untouched for the last five hundred years. These sit alongside Tudor buildings with their traditional black wooden beams running through white rendered walls. The result, described in our guidebooks as 'interesting' and 'charming' seems to me a mismatch of buildings that leave the town with no identifiable character. It's a town out of keeping with its Cotswold surrounds.

On our right is a tiny Co-op that must have had to think hard about whether to open its doors. Inside, it is dim and uninviting. A disinterested middle-aged woman sits at the front counter, and behind her are four, perhaps five rows of half-empty shelving. They display cans of vegetables, condensed milk and beef stews that might have been manufactured in the 1960s. On the left is a fridge with half a dozen coke cans and some bottled water. In the vegetable racks are three potatoes, an eggplant, randomly, and a small anaemic lettuce with wilted leaves. We turn and leave. The woman doesn't bother looking up.

The main street is no more exciting than our "rooms" or the Co-op. Again, a number of shops are boarded up with "for lease" signs displayed. Having done an uneventful lap of the main street we decide to visit the laundromat to do several days' washing. An hour and a half later, it's time for dinner so Wendy suggests a Thai spotted earlier as the most hopeful of the town's eateries. The restaurant is empty (never a good sign), but considering the lack of life here, it's understandable. Both of us order beers and focus on a decent looking menu. When the waiter approaches, we select our meals. "That's no longer available" we are told. Ok, next selection, again unavailable. After two more failed attempts I ask what exactly *is* available? He points to two chicken, one tofu and one fish dish at the bottom and says without shame; "this is all we have tonight". Orders are taken and very average food is consumed before heading back to our dreary room. Next morning, we rise early, eat a breakfast on par with the previous night's meal and leave this disappointing town behind. I make the cliché joke to Wendy that the best part of Winchcombe is the road out, and vow not to return.

My wife thinks I'm being overly critical. She admits it's not one of her favourite towns and that it *does* lack the charisma of other villages we've passed through, but thinks my impression is due to my bad mood the previous day. She reminds me that quite a lot of people *do* seem to like coming here. It has a music festival, which attracts several thousand, a walker's festival (although I'm not sure why you have a festival about walking) and is the hub for one of the Cotswold's popular pub walks. Some of the shops I refer to as derelict, she argues, are merely *quaint,* and our "barren room" is more in the vein of *minimalist.* I think she's stretching things a bit.

*A rose amongst thorns*

But the road out *is* actually the best part for one outstanding reason – Sudeley Castle. Originally built on its current site in the 1100s, the Castle you see today is slightly younger, having been rebuilt in the mid-1400s. It sits proudly still in all its splendour. The Castle is most famous of course because it marks the burial place of Katherine Parr, Henry V111's sixth and possibly most intelligent wife. She was also his most experienced, having been married twice before she gave her hand to him. Perhaps their marriage ceremony warned of times ahead, as they took their vows in the midst of one of Britain's worst plague outbreaks. Before his premature death, Henry remained deeply in love with Katherine, as she shared his interests of reading, music and debate. Her attraction to him was less convincing, as she had already intended on marrying another love – Thomas Seymour - before she was snatched by the King. After too short an interlude, Henry's ailing health caught up with him and Katherine was left a widow, for a little time at least, in this magnificent Castle. She soon went back and married Sir Thomas, but it was short-lived and less than satisfactory. She too departed the temporal world, shortly after childbirth.

The Castle is privately owned today, being the property of the 4th Baron of Ashcombe, who obviously lavished love and large amounts of cash on its upkeep. We spend several hours taking in its magnificence and touring the private rooms, which you have to say, are remarkably modest for such a well-endowed family and such royal heritage. The rooms are small, sparsely furnished and with very few modern conveniences. Given the choice, few of us would live here as it currently stands, but it is well-loved and surrounded by sumptuous gardens. There are also expansive lawns, several thousand-year-old oaks and a most glorious private lake. It certainly provides a blessed relief from the forgettable town of Winchcombe. We have, however, wittered away enough time here and I have just walked into the women's toilets by mistake, giving several elderly ladies a rather nasty surprise. I hurriedly grab Wendy by the arm and tell her not to look back.

The rest of today's official walk is quite modest. It is only supposed to be around six miles, but that is to Cleeve Hill. From what I understand, it's another hike from there to our overnight accommodation, so we want to leave plenty of time for the unexpected. There is always the *unexpected* in our walks. The climb is approximately a thousand feet, and at this point sits Belas Knap, the summit of today's adventure in more ways than one. For now, it's across another bridge, through yet another "kissing gate", and onto what looks to be a clearly defined path through the fields ahead. I feel a small surge of joy whenever the path is obvious, as it is now. Far too often it is *not*. So much of each day is spent hunting for a recognisable track or a trail sign and then making do in the absence of both. I can honestly say, I have never experienced so many false starts, doubling back, or paths that simply evaporate. But it all adds to the adventure, or so Wendy keeps telling me.

Soon, we are approaching another stream, across which we scramble before heading up to a narrow road which leads us right past Corndean Hall, an elegant ancestral home built in the early 1800s and about which little else is recorded. From here, it's a steep climb to the next plateau and the next panoramic view. Our guidebook is telling us that numerous Romans settled throughout this area some eighteen hundred years ago, capitalising on the agricultural wealth of the area. In time we will experience the remains of an intriguing Roman villa up close, but far more exciting and ancient, is the Neolithic long barrow – Belas Knap – that our trail is now approaching.

## Spying on the ancestors

Wendy and I have been looking forward to seeing Belas Knap since the beginning of the walk. Having read quite a bit about its history, the thought of actually seeing it up close and personal, I must admit, gives me a shiver. Walking in this direction you approach the barrow from its rear so that all you see is a small mound on otherwise flat ground. It's not until you circle the barrow and approach it from the front that you are met with what is the most extraordinary time portal, leading you through almost six thousand years of civilization. That's right, this Neolithic long barrow dates back to around 3,800BC. Your mind struggles not only to appreciate the number of generations that such a date represents, but you also think of the changes that each generation witnessed and participated in. You think about their beliefs, how they saw their world and adapted to it, as well as the Pagan Gods they worshipped and feared.

What was important to these early ancestors? Did they look back on their own ancestors in the same way we view them or were they ignorant of their existence? We know that they were much more in touch with their environment. They studied the seasons, the soil and the natural rhythms of their earth. But there was no science, few comforts, no written word and definitely no notion of a single God or the miracles of some fellow by the name of Jesus. All that was thousands of years into the future. In fact, their existence is almost impossible for us to fathom, as impossible as their ability to look into and imagine a future with us.

This long barrow, like most others, is an ancient, burial chamber. If you adhere to a *post ice-age hypothesis*, these long barrows were actually once ships built to carry the dead to the after-life. Their reasoning is that water levels were significantly higher then, and since the shape of the barrows so closely resembles those of sea-going vessels, this must be the explanation. I think, perhaps, if you are taken in by such a hypothesis, then fiction is probably more your thing. If you check the Latin meaning for the barrow's name, you realise that Belas means beautiful and Knap means hill, no reference to boats or water.

Anyway, its entrance, as well as the actual chamber inside (not the hull of a boat) is built from meticulously crafted stone walls and ceilings. The stones are long and narrow and placed in interlocking formation, much like the more recent dry-stone walls that now bound Cotswold properties. The entrance is about four feet high, allowing you to enter in a crouched position. Inside it is cool and dry and dark. It is eerie and exhilarating at the same time. You are, after all, entering a chamber built in the mists of time, to pay respect to the dead. I stay in my crouched position for some considerable time, stunned by the significance of this place, its palpable foothold in the history of the world.

The tomb is approximately 55 metres long and up to 26 metres wide in the middle but considering the almost six thousand years of weathering that has taken place, we can safely assume it was once much larger. To date, thirty-one human skeletons have been recovered from Belas Knap, as well as numerous animal bones. As pagans, their gods tended to represent the natural world of water, earth, fire, air, sky, and plants, possibly a more sensible belief system than some we are more familiar with. Therefore, their burial chambers were filled with the type of artefacts that they hoped would please their various gods and safeguard them into their next life. They also believed firmly in reincarnation. The interior of the barrow is surprisingly capacious and invites you to spend time here. It's a solemn, ruminative experience, one you don't forget easily. Belas Knap is indeed one of those very special places that is worthy of deep respect.

The other benefit of spending so long inside this chamber is that it gives some relief to my sunburn. It's difficult to imagine that walking in England in May could inflict an intensity of sunburn more common in Australia or California. Stupidly, I didn't bother with a hat for this journey as I expected the stereotypical English weather of grey skies and drizzle for most of the walk. So far, not a single drop has passed between the bluest of skies and the ground upon which we tread. Each night I rub moisturiser into my stinging face and neck before fronting up for another blast of sunshine the next day. The locals are every bit as puzzled by the weather as we are. No matter where you go, shops, pubs, rest rooms or B&Bs, the conversation is squarely focused on the unusual weather. Apparently, it snowed in Chipping Campden only the week before we arrived and May in this region has an average of 12 rainy days – that's almost every second day. Temperatures usually hover between 10 and 16 degrees, but currently, each day is a beautiful 20-22 degrees Celsius, and the whole month only recorded 2 days of rain. What you might call ideal walking weather.

*Inheritance real and imagined*

We can't help but notice on this walk, the sheer number of imposing manor houses and estates that seem to rise up with astounding regularity along the trail. Old, entrenched, ancestral wealth continues without disruption. Mounted on hilltops with their sweeping views of this most desirable country, each estate contains its own and the country's rich heritage. The roles they played in royal dramas, political expediency, ancestral inheritance and period architecture represents a good chunk of the nation's golden era. Fortunes were made and squandered, scandals erupted and were silenced, decisions were arrived at which affected entire generations and society at large. Their vast lawns, orchards, groves, ponds, statues and manicured gardens give some idea of the privileged lives that were lived inside their expensive walls. The upkeep on these estates alone would amount to hundreds of thousands of dollars annually. And yet, they are all beautifully maintained, still lived in, still creating history both local and national. The wealth that inhabits this region is immense.

Approaching one such estate, with a most magnificent ancestral home perched resplendently on its hill and surrounded by high, dry-stone walls, I thought I might take a peek over to see what was going on inside. I clambered up to the top of the wall and looked down straight into the face of the "owner", who was staring back up at me. "Can I help you?" he asked with some incredulity. "Sorry, sorry, just wanted to take a look at your beautiful manor" I spluttered. "Well now you have." He stared, daring me to keep looking. I jumped down and faced a highly embarrassed and not too forgiving Wendy. "Good one" she said simply and quickly turned back to the track.

It turned out that this estate is Postlip Hall, a quintessential Cotswold manor house and the gateway to the tiny hamlet of Postlip itself. As with most hamlets and villages in the Cotswolds, the manor house dominates, having once been the centre of commerce, trade and employment in that particular environ. Postlip Hall was mentioned rather a lot in the Domesday Book, its history travelling back more than a thousand years. I have to say, the house looks in remarkably good condition for its age; better than many of our contemporary houses. The hamlet is the type of place that looks like it might have featured in a children's nursery rhyme about cottage gardens, thatched-roofed houses, and warm crumpets with cream and honey.

But there is more to this place than you might think. It turns out that the hamlet is home to a long-term, social experiment, with perhaps, one or two Orwellian overtones. Sometime in the 1960s a few people who wanted to live differently, decided to get together and do something about it. Fair enough you would think. But they also decided they wanted to choose who their neighbours would be, and make sure they behaved in much the same way as themselves. Well, exactly the same way really. Sounds like the script from the American cult movie *The Truman Show*. Anyway, they have a situation that they call "private communal living".

Apparently, these guys like their own space but in a shared building. So, they bought a very large manor house and partitioned it into a number of individual dwellings. This way they could all keep an eye on each other whilst pretending to have their own privacy. They have fairly strict codes of behaviour for the community and if you're caught disobeying these codes too often it may be decided that you're not a good neighbour after all. They babysit each other's children regularly so that parents can have time away and, perhaps more importantly, to quiz the kids about family practices. There are kitchen gardens which all residents take turns in maintaining. Only wholesome, ethically acceptable vegetables are grown.

Taking a quick glance at the Postlip community website is even more unnerving. The "sixth "guideline" of their doctrine states that within their community they like "To encourage everyone to participate, even when the situation is uncomfortable for them", kind of like what happens to Winston Smith in "1984". I now realise why the fellow whose stare I met over the fence was so unfriendly. We decide to move on sooner rather than later.

## Beer and Boudicca

Today has been long and hard. The climbs have been steep and the trail all too confusing. Foolishly, Wendy and I decided to call some of the family back home while cresting the top of a steep hill. As you might expect, the calls took all our attention as we were updated on the current dramas with our children. Then it was our sisters' turn, and then our mothers. Wandering through gorgeous wooded areas, then open fields full of bright yellow rape seed, with a chorus of sweet birdsong accompanying us and all the while deep in phone conversation, we took little, in fact, no heed of the criss-crossing trails ahead. After thirty minutes in this carefree state, Wendy suddenly looks up from her phone and asks with a slightly panicked expression if I know where we are. I think she's mainly panicked by the fact that I *never* know where we are. Merely having to ask me reinforces how seriously lost we've become. Both of us stop, quickly say our goodbyes to loved ones and search hopelessly for some sort of landmark. There isn't one. On one side we are flanked by heavy woods, on the other by open fields with views to we know not where.

Cotswold trail signs are few and far between at the best of times, and now there is *nothing*. Wendy decides that we should walk in one direction for five minutes and if nothing correlates with our guidebook, we will double back and head in the opposite direction. The coverage for our phones' GPS is too patchy to make any sense so we have to rely on our wits .... always a bit of a worry. Plan A gets us nowhere. After walking in three different directions, there was still nothing that resembled our trail and the guidebook may as well have been written in Chinese for all the sense we can make of it. Then finally, when anxiety is firmly setting in we hear the glorious bark of a dog approaching. Dogs around here are always attached to their owners. And sure enough, out of the woods bounds a large German Shepherd with its owner pulled along behind. She looks rather taken aback as we rush at her gabbling in some weird Australian accent. But thankfully she is local and probably deals with strange lost types often. The woman graciously guides us back to the trail and with an amused smile sets us on our way. Thank God for Cotswold dog walkers. We came to realise, after many similar "situations," that they are always out on the trail, always know where they are, and fortunately, are willing to help clueless Australians.

The remainder of our walk today involves the long climb up to Cleeve Hill. I figure there is about another hour until we reach the Cleeve Hill Golf Club, where we leave the trail for the day and head down to our overnight accommodation in Leckhampton. This deviation turns out to be an "add-on" of three agonising miles. Wendy's feet are sore and my right knee is reminding me relentlessly of an old injury. We're both pretty well *done in*. The views on the way up are breathtaking, with uninterrupted panoramas in every direction. I'm pretty sure I can actually see Wales and can definitely recognise Gloucester. But it's that stage of the day when energy levels are low and enthusiasm even lower. Somehow, views just don't cut it at the moment. All I really want is to sit down with a cold beer before heading for a hot shower.

Standing proudly ahead of us is what locals call the "Devil's Chimney". According to legend, this marks the spot under which the Devil – "Old Nick" – used to live deep in the ground. From here, he would entertain himself by hurling large boulders down onto the township below. Unfortunately for him, the boulders had a mind of their own and hurled themselves back at him, thus burying him deep under the hill. Not your most effective brand of devil. Others believe the standing rock was carved by a farmer with a perverse sense of humour, but I think I'll stick with the unfortunate devil.

It seems much longer than the hour we calculated but finally, the roof of the Golf Club emerges above the next hill. "Thank God", sighs Wendy and our pace quickens. The original plan was to keep going until reaching Leckhampton, but it's agreed a bit of liquid sustenance is essential at this point. Walking in through the front door, we sling our packs under a table and I make a bee line for the bar. In my haste I order from the wrong tap and end up with two pints of *light* beer. I don't know what it is but when you're thirsty and in need of a quenching ale, light beer just doesn't measure up. I groan out loud, realising my mistake and a young fellow nearby immediately sidles up and asks what the problem might be. I explain and he offers to buy them from me....at a discount. He starts counting out his change, making the contrived excuse that he hasn't got as much as he thought and suggests a further substantial discount. I'm so demented with thirst that I'm considering his offer when Wendy steps in and sternly tells him it might be best if he found some other sucker to con. He sidles off again. I give her a foolish grin and suggest we take the beers out to the balcony.

We sit next to some regular punters who appear to know each other. But they happily include us in their conversation, asking us about our walk and why on earth we are doing it. They seem baffled by the idea that we want to walk the length of the Cotswolds, shaking their heads and chuckling to each other as if we might be slightly 'touched'. A middle-aged woman approaches with her large Labrador. The dog is wagging its tail but the woman is breathing hard and I must say, looks a bit worse for wear. "Hey Marj, this is the second time you've passed by in the last hour", the fellow on our right calls. Marj tells us all, and no one in particular, that she is trying to exhaust Peter (the dog, apparently) so that he won't miss them too much tonight when she and Jack head out for a curry. By the state of her, I think Jack and Peter might be the ones heading out. Everyone has another chuckle and we sip our disappointingly low-alcohol beers.

After another, more respectable beer, it's time to leave the trail and head downhill towards Leckhampton, on the outskirts of Cheltenham. The extra three miles is stretched by two wrong turns and another of Wendy's toilet stops. I figure that today's walk has ballooned to roughly 18 miles, and a lot of that, is uphill. Tonight's B&B, however, is gorgeous, decked out with snacks and full breakfast bar, comfy lounges and bed, wonderful shower and a beautiful outlook. The host, as in almost every place we've stayed, is welcoming and friendly and interested.

She seems worried that we've walked so far, as if we might suddenly collapse on her floor. She fusses around, bringing us everything that we might need while telling us to "sit and relax". We couldn't feel more at home, except there we'd be doing it all ourselves.

Heading into town after long, hot showers (despite rumours to the contrary, the English B&Bs have amazing showers), we locate an old, cheery looking pub that was built around the 1640s. I'd say, it hasn't changed much since those first stones were laid. We sit down to one of the largest meals I have ever eaten. These are washed down with a cleansing pint and then a second, and at last we both begin to feel human again. The pub is small (actually tiny) built in stone, with a lovely courtyard surrounded by gardens of roses. The folk here are well lubricated, and happy, lifting their beer in salute as you pass through. It's a wonderful atmosphere, the type that English pubs are famous for. We feel utterly content. After a large meal of very unhealthy fried food and a third ale, Wendy and I leave our new-found friends and depart for bed, feeling full and drowsy, and about as happy as we can be.

The main attraction around here is not this 1640s pub, but the annual, raucous Cheltenham Festival. Not only do thousands of locals and tourists swarm the festival in person, but millions more tune in on television, radio and online. It's one of the UK's most popular events, with seemingly good reason. Much of the crowd, both real and virtual, is there to lay bets on large animals running around a track several times and jumping over silly fences. But there is much more to the Cheltenham Festival. It coincides nicely with St Patrick's Day, so a good percentage of the crowd is made up of very proud and very drunk Irish. And their preferred tipple is, of course, Guinness, of which approximately 265,000 pints are consumed during their visit. They don't just limit themselves to this thick, meal-in-a-glass beer alone. They also drain more than 120,000 bottles of wine and a further 20,000 bottles of Champagne over the week, obviously to help dilute the beer.

And the reason why the loyal people of Cheltenham are so proud of their festival? It injects more than £100 million into their pockets each year. The thing with successful festivals such as this, is that they tend to have a self-perpetuating momentum. As they gain in popularity, they attract wider coverage, inject more into the local economy, which wins loyalty within the community. Their coverage broadens, advertising budgets deepen and even more people turn up to see what all the fuss is about. The cycle continues and the crowds swell. It is a wonderful thing. Sadly, we are here at the wrong time of year and must be content with experiencing it vicariously.

Many walking the Cotswold Way opt for the alternative overnight stay in Dowdeswell. Instead of hopping off the trail at Cleeve Hill and walking another three miles down to Leckhampton, the smarter folk stay on for a little bit and take the much more direct route to the alternative. I don't know why we didn't, but our version turned out a happy enough detour. The route to Dowdeswell takes in another Iron-Age fort, broad meadows of endless, vibrant wild-flowers, which are all opening and at their best this time of year, and a nature reserve – Chedworth - said to host thirty different species of butterfly. The reserve is only 1800 yards in length, small by nature reserve standards, but the butterflies seem to know instinctively that it's theirs, a place of safety where they can breed in peace and go about their business unmolested. The reserve now hosts a couple of very rare species and both scientists and enthusiasts from around the world come to study them.

It is also, incidentally, a place where you might spot a Roman snail. That's right. These little creatures were introduced with the Roman occupation two thousand years ago and thrive here to this day. In addition, you will find over four hundred species of rare moss growing in the area and would once have spotted the owner of Superdry, that fashionable clothing label worn by such idols as David Beckham, Brad Cooper and Idris Elba. What a wealth of wonderful species living in this tiny area. I'm not sure if there is a harmonic relationship between them all, but it's a nice thought.

# Banter in Birdlip

The good news this morning is that our wonderful host has offered to drop us back up at Cleeve Hill, where we left the trail yesterday. This saves us a good hour or so of uphill climbing, which works wonders on our mood. In no time at all Wendy and I are piling out of the car with many thank yous and farewells, and I must say, feeling rather chipper about the day ahead. Today, the track will hopefully take us to the hamlet of Birdlip, where Wendy has booked us in to the Royal George, the only accommodation in town. I always worry when the choice of accommodation is limited to one. It means they have a monopoly and often, little incentive to try. But, nothing is going to change my mood this morning. It's cold, clear, sunny and invigorating. Today's walk is also only eight miles, which after yesterday's marathon, will be a mere doddle.


After a challenging climb for the first leg of the trail our path is once again running along the plateau, providing the typically magnificent views that we have become so used to. The air up here is stunningly fresh, with a brisk, cool breeze, a strengthening Spring sun warming our bones and an altitude that lets you know you're alive. Today, there isn't even haze so that our view extends to the horizon in each direction. And looking down across this landscape of green, open fields and woods as far as the eye can see, you realise just how much of this small island is still free of human development. One of the really delightful aspects of this walk is the unadulterated panorama you are treated to each day. You don't spend your days looking at traffic or dealing with busy neighbourhoods, shopping malls or congestion. Your vista is almost entirely natural, open fields, gorgeous woods, streams and wildflowers, with every so often, the harmonious inclusion of a charming village. There is simply not the jarring of conflicting vistas that you so often experience moving between the man-made and natural world.

Soon the track descends into another wooded area, again surrounding us with carpets of bluebells and the prolific white flowers of wild garlic. We breath in deeply, filling our lungs with the sweet, strong scent. What lies around us thrills the senses, almost overwhelms them; the visual beauty, the strong scents of natural goodness, and the sweetest melodies of birdsong that complement every English wood.

In a spectrum of colour the trail soon emerges into a golden field of rape seed, just ripening and rich in its gleaming yellow/gold colours, with a pungent scent of oil hanging in the air. It stretches out before us with a narrow, waist-high path that Cotswold walkers have carved out. The crop is so high and dense that we feel as if we're floating through rather than actually walking. It's a strange sensation that only adds to our sensory barrage. And before the journey can settle into anything resembling "normal", the trail leads steeply up to the historic Crickley Hill, an ancient hill fort that archaeological finds suggest was first inhabited approximately 5,000 years ago (Neolithic). Since then, there has been continual occupation through the Bronze, Iron, Roman and Saxon ages. The latest DNA evidence also suggests that Crickley Hill was the centre of violent and prolonged assaults around 3,500 BC, with hordes of archers attacking the hillfort. You can still see the sharp ridges protruding through the ground, outlining the fort's perimeter as well as some of the structural fortifications, including the causeway, the steep and forbidding ramparts, and remains of a primary Neolithic camp.

*A metropolis it's not*

From Crickley Hill, it's down into a shallow valley and then back up onto the escarpment and into shaded woods for perhaps a mile. Fortunately, at regular intervals the woods part to allow prolonged and dramatic vistas over the county below, with its gentle undulations and vivid colours. Our trail then deviates to the road and an A-road at that. Like all A-roads in Britain, it is busy and our route follows it for about half a mile. But first, we have to navigate an enormous roundabout, which cars seem to be treating as some kind of frantic merry-go-round. It's chaos and we're right in the middle of it. Eventually, we make it to the centre island and take a breather. At this spot we look directly at the Air Balloon Pub, a place where at one stage, we had contemplated staying for the night. I can only say that the Gods must have smiled on us and directed our thinking elsewhere. Staying in a pub on this feverishly busy road, right at the junction of a roundabout, would have been hell on earth.

From here, we continue to climb up into the settlement of Birdlip, the highest altitude point of the day, at 951 feet. This is quite a change from our usual nightly descents to our resting place in one or another valley. Birdlip is your quintessential Cotswold hamlet, boasting a single, narrow road lined with three and four-hundred-year-old stone houses, reflecting that late afternoon glow as the sun strikes their stones. It's very pretty. And very, very quiet.

Birdlip has only about two hundred residents and I think every one of them believes in their tale of Celtic Queen Boudicca. She was, of course, the fearless leader who waged vicious and almost victorious war on the Roman Legions as they invaded British soil. A little more than one hundred years ago, a group of dedicated road builders was tearing up the topsoil around Birdlip, when they came across several very old looking graves. One was of a "woman" with two children. They called in a leading archaeologist and it was decided it was indeed the final resting place of the great Celt and her two daughters. Since the townsfolk knew that this was about the only thing that would put them on the map, they decided to stick with the story.

Most current historians, however, believe that it's far more likely Boudicca was buried where she fell in the West Midlands. Others say her resting place is in Leicestershire, while some believe it is in the Manchester area. One theory even claims she is buried deep under platform 10 at Kings Cross Station. There is also evidence that the body found in Birdlip is of a priest, not the queen at all, which creates a tiny problem of gender.

It seems the penchant for violent encounters might run deep in this place. Only last year, there was a report of a sordid little affair between a Birdlip mother and her technologically inept lover. The woman's husband, who received one of the amorous texts by mistake, took it upon himself to deal out some justice. After bursting into the lover's home, he crossed the room, bit the libidinous offender, stole a thousand pounds for good measure, and left.

Our accommodation here – housed in the large grey-stone Royal George - sits in a commanding position, exactly half-way along the main street, proudly announcing its monopoly on trade in the village. The establishment has a warm, welcoming glow to it. There's plenty of space among its thirty-four rooms, and a cosy, nicely furnished bar and restaurant downstairs. Having been built a mere two hundred years ago, the building is quite modern by English pub standards.

It's obvious that we're just two of a number of walkers calling this place home tonight. I suppose we should have expected that, but somehow didn't. There are about a dozen bags awaiting their owners at the foot of the stairs. These have been left by the various transport companies that take your bags from one lodging to the next each day. Mind you, they don't do it out of the goodness of their heart, some charging a hefty fee. But I have to say, the company we contracted – Carry-a-Bag – has been faultless. Our bags are picked up by 10 each morning and delivered to the next place before we arrive in the afternoon.

After showers, we enjoy a rowdy night amongst the dozen or so other walkers. There is music playing, lots of good food, swapping of trail tales and perhaps a small excess of beer. By midnight, this beer has worked its magic and we have all retired to comfy beds for a solid night's sleep.

Morning comes bright and beautiful, another clear day with lots of sunshine and the promise of a good walk ahead. Ignoring all predictions, the weather just keeps getting better. We are determined to make the most of it, getting up early, despite the increasing weariness, and setting out with a substantial lunch, plenty of bottled water, some chocolate for energy and camera batteries fully charged. There is no doubt that our fitness levels are improving dramatically. Each day's walk not only covers a good distance, but usually includes an unusual number of steep hills. The problem is, that with lots of exercise comes enormous appetites, and if I'm honest, I have to admit that the calories going in are eclipsing those being spent. Our breakfasts and lunches have been growing in size, afternoon pub stops have become more regular, and each night's dinner is nothing short of immense. We are constantly hungry and clothes are definitely feeling a little tighter. But what the heck, we're having fun.

## Of Romans and cheese

Today is a bit more eventful than anticipated. Wendy and I are heading for Painswick, a fair old hike by any standards. Even though the trail is unusually clear-cut today I'm anxious. Our guidebook tells us that soon we should notice the remains of a Roman villa off to our right and down the hill. Given our usual inability to notice the obvious, however, I pester Wendy every few yards, asking whether she thinks we may have missed it. But she follows the map assiduously, through more woods, up another hill, along a ridge and then back down, and although the remains are *not* that obvious from the trail, she manages to deliver us right to the spot.

For me, this is the most exciting part of today's walk. We are standing just above the Great Whitcombe Roman Villa and I have to say, my level of enthusiasm skyrockets. We spot the crumbling stone and brick framework outlined in the grass. It was clearly a rather substantial villa, just sitting there in the field, with no announcement or celebration. Down we head with cameras out, clicking furiously. Wendy walks around the entire perimeter taking photos from different angles while I put on my very amateurish archaeological hat and start scrabbling about in the dirt. I have no idea what I'm doing, but desperately hoping against hope to find something tantalising. Wendy just chuckles, which makes me feel even more amateurish, but I'm too excited to really care. In fact, I'm proud to say, that after about twenty minutes of searching and scratching with a by-now bent spoon, I unearth a tiny ancient-looking iron bar with some sort of symbol engraved along its edge. I'm convinced it's Roman. My day is made. I'm suddenly a fanatical archaeologist with a thirst for more. We spend another half hour in the villa with me diving on and inspecting anything that is not grass, before reluctantly heading back up to the trail for the final leg of today's walk.

Yes, I'm only one in thousands whose enthusiasm got the better of them at this villa. It is, after all, quite famous in this area and with good reason. Apparently, two millennia ago, the villa was one of the most luxurious in the region, and belonged to a wealthy family with great political influence. It contained the most intricate mosaic flooring, bath-houses, separate parlours, and colonnaded gallery. There was a large entrance-way, servants' quarters and commanding views over the surrounding countryside. When you see the villa up close and walk its perimeter, it really is quite large, even for our time, let alone two thousand years ago. From what I can gather, it was built around

AD250 and lived in continuously for the next two hundred years, until a collapsing Western Roman Empire forced the mass exodus of its citizens from Britain and just about every other country it occupied.

Most of this morning involves climbing and immediately ahead of us are some more rather challenging hills. After twenty minutes or so, the breathing is coming in quick, shallow pants with sweat breaking out in all the wrong places. Finally, I reach the top of the first hill and turn to wait for Wendy. She's taking an extended breather. Looking back down, you realise just how steep and long this particular hill is. Referring to our guidebook we suddenly realise that we're standing at the top of Cooper's Hill, the very same hill on which they hold the traditional and quite dangerous cheese rolling festival each year. This event is possibly the most exciting, and stupid activity that anybody ever dreamed up.

The idea of rolling large wheels of cheese down a very steep hill first gained traction in the early 1400s. Some romantics suggest that the Romans were the first to roll cheese down Cooper's Hill, but it's highly unlikely. You get used to the fact that around here there are many who like to credit the Romans with pretty well everything. Traditionally, these strange men and women use 9-pound balls of Gloucester cheese, which they set down at the top of the hill, then push. The usually inebriated competitors then chase the cheese down the hill. Needless to say, they rarely catch it. The drop off point of the hill is an acute 70 degrees with the cheese quickly reaching speeds of 80 miles an hour. That is, unless it bounces off track and wipes out one of the spectators, which happens regularly.

Most of the competitors end up sprawled flat on their faces at various intervals down the hill with legs failing to keep pace with either gradient or speed. The competition closes with more liquid celebration and a number of trips to the local hospital. As the madness has become more widely known, so has the participation, now from all corners of the globe. Last year alone, the number of spectators reached 15,000. There were eighteen serious injuries, eight of them participants and the other ten, spectators. In recent years one fellow broke his leg, while another poor sod dropped dead at the bottom of the hill and eight people were hit by lightening as a thunderstorm broke overhead. One year in the late 90s there were an incredible thirty-seven casualties, including a grandmother who was knocked over by an escaping cheese. Another, who jumped out of the way, ended up at the bottom of a 100-foot cliff with injuries too numerous to mention. Some might say; "only the British".

Leaving the hill, Wendy and I again have trouble finding either a path or a sign. After delivering us to the top of Cooper's Hill, the trail simply evaporates and ahead is what turns out to be a dense, confusing wood with a myriad of criss-crossing paths and no hint of anything resembling the Cotswold Way. Out comes the guidebook and in all its frustrating ambiguity it tells us to "head to the right where we will find three paths". Apparently, we should take the "most obvious one". What type of direction is that? All three paths look *obvious.* So, Wendy and I start debating what the author might mean by *obvious* and why he thinks one is more so than the other two. It's a close call, too close to spend possible hours heading in the wrong direction. I'm convinced that we clock up at least three of four extra miles a day by taking wrong turns, doubling back, searching for signs, and just getting plain lost. Finally, Wendy recommends that we take the left-hand path and, after trudging for thirty minutes, we end up back near the top of Cooper's Hill. It turns out to be one of those circular routes for people just wanting a short stroll. We *hadn't* wanted a short stroll and I made the mistake of saying so, which ensured my only company would be birds and the occasional rabbit for the next hour.

The sun is now high in the sky, a breeze gently brushing our faces, landscapes alternating between open green fields and shaded woodland, all in contrasting shades of green. Woodpeckers, wagtails, tits, goldfinches and starlings are in full and competing song. It is a truly enchanting day. Here, you feel the deep solitude of walking the Cotswold Way trail, an *aloneness* with this ancient land. It is hard *not* to fall in love with the Cotswolds, the landscape, the tiny, self-contained villages and hamlets, where life moves more slowly than the outside world, the quintessential pubs that populate each village high street, the central village green, the polite, smiling folk that greet you as you walk through their own little paradise. It's a remarkable corner of the world.

Once you get away from the tourist-focused, chocolate-box, display villages for which the Cotswolds are famously known, once you escape these and follow the trail through the *real* Cotswolds, where you participate in *living*, human and natural environments, then you really begin to appreciate the gentle beauty here. I think this is the crucial difference. You can drive through a region like this, viewing each village in turn, stepping into their myriad craft shops designed to separate you from your money. Or you can walk. When you walk, you slow the pace right down, you begin to *feel* your surroundings. You smell the different scents and listen to the chorus of far off and closer by sounds, understand the uniqueness of each tiny habitation.

*Left or right?*

We now approach another fork in the trail. Wendy is calling out that we have to take the left-hand path, which, to me would seem to take us in the opposite direction to Painswick, the village where we're staying tonight. I turn and ask if she's sure. She checks the guidebook and says "Yes, definitely to the left", but pointing to the *right*. Now I have to say from the outset, that my wife is a highly intelligent person, very intuitive. She has a sharp mind and superb analytical skills, but when it comes to coordinating directions, or relaying numbers and times, she can be profoundly confusing and confused. Not infrequently when travelling, have we ended in heated dispute after she insists that we take a left or right while pointing in the opposite direction. I invariably alert her to this incongruity, and she invariably gives me one of her cream-curdling looks and says "oh, you know what I mean, don't be so pedantic". At this point, I usually give up and take my punishment. This time I simply ask her to point in the direction she means. So, it's off to the *right* we head.

*What size is that?*

I must admit, it takes some coming to grips with just what constitutes a village or hamlet, or even a town here in Britain. Some of the villages are tiny while others seem larger than a couple of the towns we have been through. And although most hamlets are miniscule, several appear larger and busier than you would expect. To the average Australian, I think this is kind of baffling. After a little research, I'm even more confused. One site tells me that to be a *city* in Britain you have to have a cathedral or a university. There is also a clear distinction between *church* and *cathedral.* For a *town,* you must have a market. For a *village* you won't have either a cathedral or a market but must have a church.

In the case of a *hamlet,* size is a crucial factor. Hamlets usually only contain a handful of houses. They may or may not have a church but normally won't have any shops or other services.

Meanwhile, good old Wikipedia tells me that, depending on jurisdiction and geography, a *hamlet* may be the size of a village, town or parish but definitely does not have a church. Another site says that the definitions are completely size dependent and yet another tells me that it all depends on the amount of services being offered. Interestingly, the more precise measure of "population" is never mentioned. So, take your pick, but I think I'll stick with size, as the other definitions seem to confuse rather than clarify.

We are now entering Painswick, which by my reckoning, is a village. I just hope this particular village has a pub that sells large mugs of beer. Walking this trail is much thirstier work than either of us had expected and the ale here is better than either of us anticipated. We find, not a pub, but a much less common "bar" that happens to be perched high up in the village with a romantic, wisteria-covered balcony. Quickly commandeering this balcony, we set ourselves up in comfortable chairs "borrowed" from the inside lounge.

I'm sure most of you have had the experience when, after a long walk or some other exhausting exercise, you sit in a beautiful spot with your favourite tipple and relax into an almost catatonic state of blissful fatigue. We're experiencing that right now, working our way through two sweet pints of the best British ale, and looking out across a sea of mauve and pink wisteria to green fields and small stone cottages beyond. It is sublime. I wonder if this might be the closest to heaven I get. Wendy looks across at me and gives that deliciously dreamy smile that only a profoundly satisfied person can give. After a lengthy reverie, we finally shake ourselves back to reality. It's time to lift our creaking bones and head to tonight's accommodation.

# Four in the Doll's House

Painswick, it turns out, is a very pretty village indeed. It has been built, as is usual in the Cotswolds, on the wealth of wool. From Painswick Beacon, the site of an Iron-Age hill fort, you are treated to the most splendid views across the Severn Valley to the Welsh mountains beyond, a truly magnificent sight on a clear day like today. It seems that every hilltop, every plateau, introduces you to an array of spectacular views that stop you in your tracks.

*Sunshine and scandal*

The village was chosen a couple of years back as the location for the film adaptation of J.K. Rowling's "A Casual Vacancy", which wasn't quite the stellar hit that her Harry Potter series has been, but entertaining enough. The three-part series was claimed by many around the country to be a politically-motivated exercise in Tory-bashing. But most residents in Painswick believe the director got it pretty right in his depiction of the scandals behind quiet village life.  Even more scandalous, was the introduction of a somewhat raunchy lingerie shop. It was designed and built exclusively for the show's production but a number of Painswick's more sensitive folk thought it was the real deal.

They got together and sent of a torrent of highly incensed letters to the parish council demanding its immediate closure.

According to one resident, the sweet façade of Painswick covers "too many scandals to mention". Not least by the village's postmistress; she recently appeared in court on eight charges of theft. She claims she stole a jacket from a parcel to get *out* of custody, not sure how that worked. And she went on to steal a Blackberry phone because her solicitor apparently *told* her to. The Royal Mail didn't believe these stories either and tested her by tracing two parcels for which she was responsible. Not surprisingly, the one containing a valuable carriage clock went missing. She's still claiming her innocence.

It seems scandal has been plaguing this village for some time too. Back in the early years of the twentieth century when Freemasonry was in its prime, one of its leaders brought notoriety on himself, his business and his secretive society. News has it that he was having trouble restricting his amorous activities to his wife, so took up with her sister as well. The end result was fathering fifteen children by his wife and another ten by his mistress. All this productivity came to nought, however, when the village disowned him. He lived out his years in deep shame.

On a brighter note, the village has welcomed its newest resident – singer/songwriter Lily Allen. She fell in love with this charming place a little while back, apparently thrilled by the village cricket, the pubs and the homemade lardy cake. She got so excited, in fact, that she spent a cool £3 million on a 17$^{th}$ century, six-bedroom house just out of town. Here, she can be close to London, lose herself in the winding, cobbled streets of picturesque Painswick as well as rub shoulders with the likes of Hugh Grant, Damien Hirst and other fly-in, fly-out celebrities.

Reflecting the classic English penchant for unsettling outsiders, "New Street" in Painswick has actually been around since the early 1400s, and most of the cottages lining it are at least four or five hundred years old. Several of the occupants we see emerging from these wee dwellings seem only just shy of that age themselves. They shuffle along the footpath just as their parents, grandparents and great-grandparents did before them. It's a multi-generational village with family histories reaching back to the eleventh century. As with many villages here, there is a grand church near the centre of town that dominates its surroundings. This particular one is very large and very graceful and has an extended courtyard the covers several acres. It also has a rather unusual collection of beautifully manicured Yew trees; in fact, ninety-nine of them. These trees are a form of conifer that is often referred to as "the Tree of the Dead", I think because they tend to outlive those who planted them. They actually achieve great age, with many planted by Saxons still thriving, and several having reached an estimated age of 3,000 years. That's a lot of history stored in those mighty trunks.

The Yew trees here in Painswick are a smaller variety and have been shaped and clipped meticulously. They have been planted and trained to line the eight or so paths leading to the church, creating archways that form geometric patterns across vast lawns. They just invite you to walk among them. You can't help it. When you come across a sight like this, with trees so obviously ancient, cared for and loved, standing proudly in formations you feel a need to get amongst them, and so we did.

It's with some difficulty that we cross one of the one busier streets in Painswick. It's a "B-road" and for some reason runs right through the centre of town carrying a constant stream of workers, tourists, salesmen and others who just like driving through sleepy villages. Step fifty feet to either side and you are back in a quiet, sleepy village, but approach this river of cars and you have to have your wits. Our accommodation for the night is across this road and up the hill on the left. It's classed as a "B&B", but there is only one room in the main house, reserved for the travelling salesmen. To the rear of the house, across a tiny but pretty yard there is more accommodation in the form of stand-alone apartments.

Knocking on the door to the main house, we're greeted with a very business-like "good-afternoon." It comes in a broad Newcastle accent belonging to a thin, white-haired, 50-something woman who finds it difficult to smile. After a brutally brief introduction she bombards us with a list of instructions (mostly what *not* to do) before we even make it into the hall. Both Wendy and I are beginning to have serious misgivings about our choice. But as soon as we're inside, the woman's manner changes completely. She morphs into a hospitable, personable host who, for the next twenty-four hours, does everything in her power to fulfil our wishes. I want to tell her that it might be a good idea to change her style of greeting, but I'm afraid her attitude might regress rather too quickly for my liking. Instead, I keep my mouth shut and let Wendy, the far more diplomatic of us, do the talking.

The host provides a rapid but comprehensive verbal list of what is where, the best restaurants, breakfast schedules, and where the best ales might be had. Then, in her no-nonsense way, she leads us to what will be our apartment for the night. On entering, my first thought is how much time and trouble this woman has taken to make the place welcoming. It is generously provisioned and thoroughly comfortable. My second thought is how relieved I am that she's not decorating our house. Everything is just a bit trite, a bit overdone, and a bit too pretty. It is like entering a very large doll's house. Nevertheless, it's a warm and comfortable dolls house. And, I have to say, it has the best bed we've had all trip. After a typical pub meal of roast meat and vegies, washed down with a couple of their best bitters, sleep comes quickly and luxuriously.

Breakfast next morning is as sumptuous as the bed last night. There are choices of cereal, porridge, toast, bacon, eggs, mushrooms, sausages, baked beans, every condiment imaginable and freshly squeezed orange juice. And there are lashings of everything, so much so that I feel I should move carefully for the next hour or so. As our host brings my second cup of coffee, she asks if we are familiar with the reality show "Four in a Bed"? Wendy has never heard of it but it just so happens I know it quite well. Some years ago, I stumbled across it on one of our Pay TV channels and became hooked for half a season. In a nutshell the show is centred around four couples who own or manage B&Bs. They take turns to stay at each other's B&B and then rate it on everything from cleanliness, to customer service, to friendliness and comfort levels. The B&B that scores the most points by the end of the show, is presented with a "winner's certificate" and promoted through the show's advertising. After I admit my familiarity, our host proudly announces that she has just won the latest contest. She also tells us in no uncertain manner that the episode she is in airs tonight. We are expected to tune in. We do and immediately realise how much people change when put in front of a TV camera. I'll say no more.

## Champagne and thunderstorms

Today's destination is Selsley West. As far as I can tell, there's no Selsley East, North or South, just West. Whatever it is, it promises to be a long walk. So, after a monstrous breakfast and swift goodbyes to our *back-to-business* host, we head out early with heavy backpacks. Today suggests rain at some stage so we'd like to get as much walking done as possible before the weather changes. We have also packed substantial lunches to sustain us through the longer than usual afternoon.

I look across at Wendy to see her chuckling and ask what the joke is. "I just love your dress sense," she quips. "On this walk so far, you have changed from one dark-red T-shirt to another and from one fawn set of walking pants to another. Ever thought of being a bit adventurous and mixing up the colours?"

"I like these", I say.

She laughs again. "That's obvious".

I must admit I take a lot less trouble and thought about dressing each morning than does Wendy. Each day is a new dress experience for her. She constantly mixes and matches and never seems to be in the same thing twice. And, she always looks good.

By 10.am, the day is already becoming warm, very warm. With the gradual build-up of clouds in the west, I'm thinking we may *well* have rain this afternoon, probably in the form of a thunderstorm. Right now, though, water bottles are being drained and sweat is running freely. Wendy points to what looks like a small gathering of people on the track in the distance and we realise they're the first walkers we have seen for two days. Many of the walkers we came across at the beginning have since faded away. Now, it's mostly the two of us in solitude, which suits me fine. But as we draw closer this gathering appears quite large. Eventually, they are before us and not one of them would be under seventy. There must be twenty of them standing in a semi-circle with glasses of Champagne in hands, right in the middle of the track. They are laughing and joking and generally having a grand old time. Good on them I think, but why?

Well, it turns out that this same venerable group of walkers, or ramblers as they call themselves, has been meeting every month. Each time, they meet at a different location somewhere in the south of England, and, for longer than any of them can remember, walk the myriad trails on offer. Today, they are celebrating because they have just clocked up their five thousandth mile together. By anyone's book that'ss a pretty impressive feat. And by the look of the empty champagne bottles lying around, and their rosy cheeks, they think so too. We stay and help celebrate for a while, take some group photos and as we leave I wish them good luck for the next five thousand miles. One of the old fellows calls back, "no chance of that, we'll all be dead" and gives a wry laugh.

It must be the day for outings because not more than a mile· further along we come across two ageing women in full walking gear, sitting on a bench overlooking the most spectacular view you can imagine. Again, a short chat is expected. They tell us they often take walks together along this track and try to find a nice bench on which to park themselves for morning tea. By the size of their 'morning tea', which includes cup-cakes, chocolate slices and custard tarts, and the way their sweaters stretch across their middles, I'd say they focus a fair bit more on the morning teas than the walking.

*The one-man village*

This area is also famous for a single man, from a single village. Laurie Lee, the celebrated writer, lived at different stages of his life in the Cotswold village of Slad. He wrote a famous bestseller – "Cider with Rosie" - about life in Slad, which put the village fairly and squarely on the tourist map. The book was more an autobiography than musings about the village but that didn't stop the Tourist Bureau cashing in. Many a visitor to the Cotswolds over the last twenty years has made a bee-line for this place and more particularly, the Woolpack Inn, which Lee is known to have frequented to drink with friends. Some, including myself, find the book curiously uninteresting. The distinguished historian, Tom Fort implies that it paints a somewhat myopic portrait of a working village through the eyes of a non-working and perhaps slightly spoilt, man-child. Still, that hasn't stopped it being a bestseller for many a year and a lucrative drawcard for tourist dollars.

They have even turned the book into a TV show and the village has gone to the trouble of laying a five-mile "Laurie Lee" nature walk around its perimeter, interrupted with 'poetry posts' in Lee's honour. Such posts are sadly ironic. Whilst Lee is indeed a celebrated writer, he never quite made it as a poet. To his lasting dismay, his poems didn't ever enjoy the success he hoped for them and it was only after he failed at this first love that he turned to writing books. But, given that the vast majority of tourist slogans today are at least partly mythical, why quibble about this particular one? Just don't expect Slad to be another chocolate-box Cotswold village, because its aesthetic qualities are nothing to get excited about.

## Hated history

Not far from the bench upon which our two food lovers were seated is the Cromwell Stone. For such a hated man in English history, there are certainly enough reminders of his life and deeds. I suppose if you cause as much mayhem and destruction as this fellow did, you are going to impact a lot of national and local history, and, in some perverse way, be remembered for it. This particular stone was constructed in 1645 to commemorate the siege of Gloucester. The siege was one of the first in the English Civil War between the Parliamentarians and the Royalists, and came soon after the fall of Cirencester. It was simply the next stepping-stone in Charles I's consolidation of power. Gloucester was of particular interest because it straddled one of the main supply routes for food, ammunition, water and uniforms and therefore, controlled whether the King had an army or a dispirited bunch of deserters.

When Oliver Cromwell was finally killed, his head was impaled on an extra-long spike, and because of the intense hatred for him, it stayed that way for the next twenty years. But the horror didn't stop there. Such was the fear and loathing of the man that even the devil was called in for an appearance. It was said among many at the time, that on the night Cromwell was killed, Britain was besieged by one of its fiercest ever storms, one that wreaked widespread devastation and caused misery for months to come. Its severity was the consequence of an infuriated devil, coming to claim Cromwell's soul for safekeeping. And, if you read the Cambridge News, you might believe that the ghost of Cromwell still haunts us. Apparently two visitors to his house in Ely were filming inside when an orb of his head passed just inches from their face and then disappeared. One suspects, however, the ghost may have had more to do with the two visitors having just emerged from a long lunch at the King's Arms.


*What are they thinking?*

After another of Wendy's toilet stops, we start the final leg towards Selsley West. It has been long and hard and our legs are protesting with every step. We're taking the alternative route today. Instead of the direct trail to King's Stanley, we thought, for some inexplicable reason that it might be nice to try the alternate, longer trail. It adds a couple more miles, much of which we spend climbing.

There *are* some unexpected sights though. Right now, in front of us is an English vineyard. I have spent quite a bit of time in vineyards, almost always located in hot valleys with steep hills, where the grapes get some serious sunlight. But coming across one in the middle of the Cotswolds is a novelty indeed. I know that starting vineyards in previously unexplored places is very much the fashion, but here in a usually cold, rainy Britain it's pushing the boundaries a bit. Even more perversely, this vineyard has irrigation pipes running through its length and breadth. Despite claims to the contrary, vineyards in even the hottest, driest climates don't need any more water than they receive from the heavens. So, to put irrigation in an English vineyard almost feels like they're having a bit of a joke.

When William conquered this little island in 1066, there *were* vineyards up and down the length of the country producing almost reasonable wine, but the average temperature back then was a good ten degrees warmer than today. And perhaps with global warming we might get back there, but I really think these guys might be jumping the gun. What's worse, they're growing red wine grapes, which I can tell you, take a lot of extended heat if they're going to produce anything worth drinking. I have tasted some red varieties from cold regions and the best place to put them is in your fuel tank. Still, it's a pretty vineyard and sets the landscape off nicely, just not sure I'll be rushing in to sample their product.

Wendy and I have now been walking for many hours and although we only had lunch about two hours ago, I'm looking for an excuse to take another break. We find one when walking downhill to a winding, tree-lined canal below, where the track diverges to Selsley West. Pretending I want to take in the gorgeous scenery I suggest a snack break on the canal's banks. It is enchanting here, sitting on the edge of the tow path with the long, narrow canal stretching away to either side of us, giant willows lining both banks, ducks guiding their young upstream, several elegant herons watching us with interest and even a couple of swans gliding through deep reflections. There is a soft chorus of birdsong from the surrounding woods and no other human in sight. An atmosphere perfect for a bit of meditation, if only we had the energy to cross our legs and concentrate.

Instead, we lie back onto the tow path and munch our muesli bars, trying not to fall asleep.

This particular stretch of water is the Stroudwater Canal, the very first canal connecting the Thames and Severn rivers. Opened in 1779, its total length is around thirty-six miles, and by most standards is both broad and deep. As with most UK canals, now numbering one hundred and three with a combined length of more than three thousand miles, it was originally designed and built to move cargo. Coal, wood, textiles and various other bulk materials were carried on long narrow boats into and out of large cities and towns during the momentous Industrial Revolution. For many, this movement of cargo became a way of life. Most of the narrowboat owners lived on the canal in small, cramped quarters either fore or aft of the boat's cargo holds. It was not in the least bit romantic or peaceful. Tight timelines were in force, pay was low and intermittent, hours were long, and travel was slow and arduous. Narrowboats back then did not have motors but instead, were pulled by miserable, overworked horses. Life was hard, dirty and exhausting.

Today of course, it's a completely different story. Leisure is the name of the game on Britain's canal network. Yes, there are still working boats and people can make a meagre living from hauling cargo. But those lifestyles have largely been lost. Today canals are as popular, if not more so than they ever have been but it's all about fun. There are myriad canal conservation and restoration clubs covering the length and breadth of Britain, and they do a wonderful job. In fact, it's these clubs that are largely responsible for the mass rejuvenation of the canal network and the nation's renewed enthusiasm for its use.  In the last ten years alone, more than 32,000 narrowboats have used Britain's canals, the majority carrying day-trippers or those on a weekly canal vacation. It is hugely popular, with people often forced to book the rental boats months in advance. The more prominent canals resemble busy highways during summer. In addition, hundreds of thousands of walkers use the canal tow paths to take their daily exercise, on routes that allow them to think they're getting away from it all. Here, though, there is just one old, sleepy narrowboat dawdling up the canal and three more moored to the bank opposite. It's about as peaceful as you can get.

At last, after what has seemed a marathon walk our village of Selsley West is visible. Soon, a quick stop-off at the Sainsbury

Superstore (I do love their supermarkets) will be called for. Supplies for dinner, including a nice bottle of red (Spanish and non-irrigated) are needed. Wendy has found what she believes is a short cut. She leads the way along a narrow path beside a trickle of a stream. The path quickly loses itself in thick brambles and malevolent thistles before disappearing altogether. Soon the brambles morph into a large, incredibly pungent rubbish tip from which we find it difficult to escape. There are old tyres, discarded clothes, piles of rotting food and generally, whatever people can think of that they no longer want. It's difficult to escape the stench. On one side it's lined by steep greasy banks, and on the other, the stream. Eventually, Wendy spots the path leading out from the bank and across a bridge into town. Climb the greasy bank we must. Twenty minutes later we enter the clinically cavernous foyer of a Sainsbury's Superstore.

Backpacks overflowing with food and wine, it's time to tackle the final, and what feels like unreasonably steep hill into Selsley West, where our apartment awaits. No sooner are we in the door and collapsed on the lounge when a loud clap of thunder announces heavy rain. Down it comes for the next thirty minutes, the first rain of the walk and perhaps a harbinger of what's to come.

# Confusion and compulsion

Our apartment is stunning, a self-contained luxury pad on the ground floor of a Cotswold manor house. The owners are away, the wife in California and the husband at his merchant bank in London. Absentee owners are a common occurrence in English villages nowadays. Particularly in these pretty Cotswold villages, the trend is for wealthy Londoners to buy a property for a bit of the good life on weekends. During the week, they either endure long commutes, or if they're sufficiently loaded, have their London pad to bunk down in Monday to Friday.

The Telegraph tells us that an astonishing 10% of British adults own a second home (well actually the bank does) and only a small proportion of them rent these places out. Most prefer to use them as holiday homes or weekenders. The claim is wrong. A little more research tells me that the figure is more like 2.8%. Nevertheless, it's still a lot of people. This research claims that indeed, most of these second or third homers *are* from London and own a good percentage of the homes in the Cotswold area as well as coastal paradises such as Cornwall. I can almost understand this national obsession, particularly among people wanting to escape the madness of London. But I can't help thinking it might be more economical if these people just unloaded their expensive lifestyles and debt-laden possessions, sold up everything and bought a simple, full-time pad in the country. This way, they might *really* get in touch with their roots. Just a thought, mind you.

Another thought is the cruel irony of second homers wanting to obtain some of that special village life for themselves. By seeking the idyllic Cotswold culture they threaten its very existence. Cotswold lifers are up in arms, with good reason, about these Londoners snapping up every available property, then leaving them vacant for 70% of the time. This, they claim, not only prices locals out of the market, but undermines the cultural and social fabric of the village. Properties are increasingly owned by absentee residents who aren't around to participate in village life. Locals are increasingly surrounded by neighbours they don't know. Village social, craft and school associations no longer have the numbers to remain viable. The community suffers as fewer residents know one another or socialise in a meaningful way. Before long, they claim, their homely, close-knit village will become just another amorphous group of houses in which residents (and non-residents) keep to themselves. The idyllic Cotswold village will cease to exist. The dream will be shattered.

I don't think there are many second-homers in Selsley West mind. Most of the residents here look to be long-term, stern-faced and very much entrenched in their tiny Anglo-Saxon stronghold. It's a quiet village with not a lot going on. Surrounded by the beautiful green pastures that dominate much of the Cotswolds, there is one pub, one main road that winds steeply up a long hill, and about a hundred cottages in total. It's as opposite to London as you could get.

But enough hypothesising for now. Tonight at least, we are Lords of the Manor and with the amount of food and wine we have purchased, we intend to feast in style. After showers and a change of clothes we set about cooking dinner in the palatial kitchen. A hearty meal, washed down with far too much wine guarantees that our weariness soon overwhelms. We don't even have enough energy for television. Instead, it's off to the house-sized bedroom and king bed.

There is one real problem with being on the move all the time. When you're sleeping in different cottages each night and are in that middle-aged bracket in which *senior moments* occur with alarming regularity, you *can* become rather disorientated at night. Sometimes I wake and wonder where the hell I am. I have to lie still counting each stop to work out exactly where we are. Then I have to work out where in the house I am and *always*, the direction of the bathroom. Several nights ago, I had woken to visit the bathroom and made a very wrong turn. Thinking I was in another place altogether, I hauled myself out of bed and walked into the linen cupboard before realising it wasn't the best place to relieve myself. Tonight, I get up and walk straight into the wall. Hitting it with an almighty thump, I fall back into bed, giving Wendy the fright of her life.

I'm not alone, however, when it comes to accidents. Apparently in Britain the most common cause of death, along with road accidents, is by people falling down their stairs. An astounding 33% of Brits admitted to falling down stairs in the past twelve months. In fact, there is a stair fall every 90 seconds in the UK, with 787 deaths recorded in 2015 alone. There's more chance of dying from a stair fall than being run over by a car, electrocuted or drowned, being assaulted or being hit by a falling object. More than 60% of these staircase accidents were among the elderly, of which 100,000 are treated every year for injuries sustained on (or off) the stairs. Those in the north-east of the country seem particularly accident-prone, with 48% recording serious falls. I'm not sure why this is. Perhaps the colder weather up there requires higher staircases to access more warmth or they just drink more before approaching them. Whatever the cause, it's clear that using your stairs at home is an incredibly dangerous business. There should be staircase life-insurance.

For me, this begs the obvious question of why so many British houses have two floors. Why increase your odds of instant death just so you can sleep upstairs? More surprising still are the number of people over 70 who, when looking for a new home, don't even flinch at buying a two-story house. What's going to happen to these poor sods when they hit 80 or 90? I guess they either live downstairs or risk death on a daily basis. It's not really a lot to look forward to. Yes, warm air rises and in a cold climate like Britain, it's easier to keep warm upstairs than down. But it seems to me these people place a lot more importance on staying warm than on staying alive.

*Man's best friend*

The Brits' obsession with two storey houses is matched only by their love of dogs. If the four-legged canine is universally seen as man's best friend, then in Britain they are positively revered. Almost everywhere you go, towns, villages, walking trails, shops, pubs, cafes, even restaurants, you will come across people of all ages with their beloved dog. A few nights ago, a couple across the road from us were obviously packing their car for holiday and the final piece of luggage they threw in, was the family dog. These creatures hold pride of place in most families across Britain and accompany their owners everywhere. There seems to be no question of actually leaving your dog at home. They just go where you go. Most dogs in England sleep indoors and many in the owner's bedroom, some even on the bed. They are cherished beyond all other pets and often above other family members. If you pay attention to a dog over here, you are immediately on closest of terms with its owner. They greet you with a warm smile and want to engage you in conversation. If you actually bend down to pat the dog, then consider yourself invited home for a meal. In fact, most of our introductions to English people on the trail are through their dogs.

Archaeology tells us that at least five hundred thousand years ago, the predecessors of man were training wolves to help them hunt. Then, during the Stone Age, their taming became broader and more sophisticated, including farm work, hunting a greater range of animals, and other chores. Their selective breeding over millennia has resulted in a domestic animal now known as the humble dog. Romans were the first, as with so many initiatives, to own dogs as actual pets and walked them on a regular basis as well as rewarding or cajoling them for certain behaviours.

According to the latest poll, there are now 8.3 million of these beloved creatures in the UK and I would say it's a pretty fair bet that each one of them enjoys as many - if not more - luxuries than its owner. The Daily Star tells us that the average British dog owner takes his or her pooch on 433 walks a year. Most of them also hold conversations with their pet while on such walks. When not talking *to* them, they talk to others *about* them. And, according to this paper, owners enthusiastically spend vast sums of money on various treats, special kennels, grooming and even holidays for their pooches. There are no lengths to which the British dog owner won't go to make their pet feel special.

*Dawdling to Dursley*

After a night of comatose sleep, this morning we awaken to grey skies and light drizzle. It is cold and a bit miserable all round, and we would much prefer to curl up in bed for the day with a good book or some trashy TV. Our bones are weary and neither of us feels the least bit like walking through this grey wet. But push on we must. As usual, our route out of the village is all uphill. It's a long climb to the plateau above Selsley but again, the view is worth it. We look right across the Stroud Valley with acres of green fields, speckled with half a dozen tiny hamlets hugging the hills, and the canal snaking its way in between them. The monotony of beauty becomes quite anesthetising.

Naturally, when we look for the trail there are four of them and not a sign in sight. "Take your pick", Wendy says. I suddenly remember a great Churchill quote – "Success is going from failure to failure without loss of enthusiasm". So, we really *do* pick one of the tracks at random and try our luck. Fortunately, after ten minutes walking, it turns out by some miracle to be the right one. More excitingly, it leads us directly to the Nympsfield Long Barrow. It too, contains intriguing kernels of human development and a history littered with remarkable feats but visually, it has nothing on Belas Knap. In fact, there are so many barrows and hill forts dotting Britain that they become a bit like cathedrals. You come across them so often that the experience can numb your senses if you let it. There are at least forty long barrows in the Gloucester county alone. You have to keep reminding yourself of their significance in terms of history and civilisation. You have to remember how fortunate you are to be here, among them, participating in that history, witnessing their march through time.

As it turns out, the Nympsfield Barrow is a mere whipper snapper in archaeological terms, only dating back to the New Stone Age (2,500 BC). The average age of long barrows around here is about 5,500 years, with a couple of the really ancient ones reaching back 8,000 years. Nympsfield was first excavated in 1862, when they uncovered thirteen Neolithic skeletons as well as numerous shards of pottery and eating utensils. I love the way these monuments and relics just sit in fields with no fuss, just there for you to stumble across on your walk. I suppose that's what makes this land so special. It is packed full of incredibly ancient remains that are available to everyone. You can spend as long as you like investigating or just staring in wonder, or even picnicking amongst them. Whatever takes your fancy.

## Aged Royally

Approximately 15 miles to our right is the royal spread that Charles and Camilla inhabit. Situated near the Cotswold village of Tetbury, Highgrove House is gorgeous by any standard. Since Charles moved in almost forty years ago, he has pursued his passion for all things organic, transforming the Estate's gardens. He has done a spectacular job. They are completely organic but also visually splendid, as well as 'innovative and sustainable' if you believe the PR. The Gardens and House receive more than 30,000 visitors a year, who are able, encouraged even, to purchase from an array of bewildering products. You can start off with a tour, at £26 per head. If you want to lash out and make Charles happy, you can opt for a private champagne tour for a mere £185. When that's whetted your appetite, you might pop into the gift shop and purchase from a selection of food and estate-sanctioned wines, garden equipment, seedlings, and seeds. There are also mugs, and other assorted crockery, bed linen, towels, bath soaps, retirement gifts and stationary. The selection is random and endless, and I assume, goes a long way towards paying for the army of gardeners.

Charles and his mum only purchased the house in the 1980s. He then renovated extensively, sustainably and expensively before launching his organic crusade on the rest of the Estate.

Nowadays, he flits by helicopter between Princess Anne's pad six miles away, Will and Kate's modest abode in Kensington, and his mum's, wherever she might be at the time. When that gets a bit monotonous he visits his other 1100 acres nearby, where he experiments with organic principles on a somewhat larger scale.

The single most noticeable consequence of Charles and Camilla residing in this area, is the extraordinary demand on real estate. Agents will regularly advertise houses in the immediate region of Highgrove as "within the desirable neighbourhood of Highgrove", or "Opportunity to be Prince Charles' neighbour". Of course, the house price premium jumps dramatically the closer you get to the Estate. And that's in the already stratospheric property market of the Cotswolds. While the average UK property price languishes at close to £226,000, a level at which it has been hovering for some years, the Cotswold property average is £510,000. What's more, over the past 12 months property prices across the UK rose by a modest 2.2%. In London, they actually fell by 0.4% in the same period. They jumped by10.5% in the Cotswolds. That's one heck of a premium.

Our destination today is not really in Charles' league, or, for that matter, the rest of the Cotswolds. After another hour's walking through beautiful but eerie woodland, in which thick-set trees seem to close around and lock us in, it begins to rain. We are drawing to the close of a long day and legs and feet are aching. I'm almost ready to call it a day when the view opens up to a truly awful sight. Ahead, the trail is leading in an arrow-straight line, right to the base of the highest hill we have seen for some time. The hill is Cam Long Down and rises ominously from the flat plain between us and it. Worse, for the first time on this walk, the trail isn't winding backwards and forwards on itself in order to take the longest route. Instead, it's leading directly up the centre of the hill in a tortuous incline. We just stare at it, then turn and stare at each other. Wendy lets out a simple but appropriate expletive and trudges on ahead. I heave my pack, mutter something melodramatic, and follow. Twenty minutes later, including numerous breaks to catch ragged breath, we are wet, tired and fed up. From the top of the hill you enter a meandering trail that winds its way across the plateau for quite some way, but at last there is the gratifying view of Dursley, down below. Another twenty minutes and we are in the heart of town.

I'm not sure who chose this name but it originated in the Anglo-Saxon era and it's rather an unattractive one. It sounds even more unpalatable when you think of its namesake in the Harry Potter series, the despicable Vernon, Petunia and Dudley Dursley whom Harry is unfortunate enough to have as relatives and minders. The town itself was once a manufacturing centre for all sorts of textiles but by the middle ages was reduced to a market town, servicing not much more than agricultural requirements. Its history dates back to the Roman invasion in AD 43, and in the middle ages had quite a bit of royal blood running through it. There were strong links to Edward the Confessor and Roger de Berkeley, who made the town his own, building his Manor just in time to be counted in the Domesday Book. Roger was the Feudal Baron of Dursley and his "Manor" was more a castle. He ruled this town with an iron fist.

The de Berkeley's were not quite trusted by the natives of Dursley as they believed Roger got on rather too well with King William and his fellow Normans. Although he was officially Lord of Dursley he was never as accepted as he would have liked. Fortunately, his stranglehold on the town only lasted until the 1170s when King Henry II took a decided dislike to the man and removed him from his tenure and with brutal efficiency. The de Berkeleys thus passed into history and the townsfolk got on with reversing most of Roger's initiatives.

But did the de Berkeley's ever quite leave? The de Berkeley Castle is still recognised as one of the most haunted places in the Cotswolds, due largely to it being the scene of a grisly royal death. As it happens, King Edward II was held in the Castle's dungeons for several months, treated with contempt and scorn and half starved before being put to death by Queen Isabella. She thought it a novel idea to kill him herself. She also chose the rather sadistic method of inserting a red-hot poker into various orifices until the shock and pain rendered him unconscious and finally killed him. Each year on the anniversary of his death his screams for mercy can still be heard throughout Dursley and the valleys beyond. The Middle Ages, of course, were turbulent times. This type of alternating ascendency to power was usually followed closely by betrayal and revenge. The trick was to get rid of all your enemies before they got rid of you. But often, your friends didn't really appreciate loyalty either. And so, complacency was never an option.

*Bursting at the seams*

Today, Dursley has a bustling town square with an outdoor hall that hosts weekly Farmers Markets, a busy street running either side of this hall, and rows of shops, cafes, and co-ops. Further along the main street, is one of the largest retirement villages I have come across. It is neither a pleasant nor unpleasant town, just a relatively non-descript settlement that is lively but doesn't share the prettiness of the other Cotswold villages.

What we *do* notice, however, is the number of middle and late middle-aged residents with some form of self-induced disability. Never have we seen so many people under seventy that have such trouble moving from one spot to the next. They're on walking sticks and frames, in wheelchairs, on motorised scooters or just plain sitting. I can't help but take a close interest in these people, as there's no indication of any serious health issues except their weight. This single problem seems to have disabled quite a bit of the town.

*Tiny tots*

Right now, however, there are more pressing matters on which to focus. Wendy directs us to our B&B for the night, where we're welcomed in by a delightful woman who is also one of Dursley's middle-aged, but slim, mobile and healthy. Also greeting us at the door are her two very large dogs, who try to outdo each other lavishing us with attention. The first one, a great Dane, jumps straight up and lands his huge paws on Wendy's shoulders, pinning her against the wall. The second one barks and does the same to me. "Hope you don't mind dogs" the host says with a smile.

She pleasantly but firmly suggests that we sit in the lounge while she prepares coffee and biscuits for afternoon tea (I'm getting the impression that B&B hosts are used to giving orders). After making room for the dogs who insist on sitting with us, we take time to look around the four-hundred-year-old cottage. This place has character on steroids – the ceiling slants, none of the walls are straight or line up correctly, the floor rises and falls at random intervals, and pretty well everything creaks. As our host returns with refreshments, I comment on her exquisite, character-filled home. She beams at me and tells us she had her eye on it for years, hoping it would come up for sale, so when it did, she snapped it up. With that, she gives us a tour of the place.

The cottage extends over three flights of stairs to more crooked rooms and slanting ceilings but it's far larger than it looks from the outside. The stairs are steep, narrow, and feel rather unsafe. And, as luck would have it, our room is at the very top – a gorgeously decorated, well-equipped, shoe-box of an attic.

I have to say that Wendy and I are by no means tall. Even so, we each have to bend down to enter the room. Our bags, which the host had kindly brought up earlier, take up a large chunk of available space and we have to bend into odd angles to get around the bed to the window and then from the window to the door. Wendy casts me an apprehensive glance that lets me know she's not looking forward to my nightly bathroom visits. Neither am I if I'm honest. After a mediocre Mexican meal in town and a walk along the main street to check on non-existent nightlife, we head back to our miniature attic and attempt to get into bed. It takes some time. The ceiling height is no more than five feet and the bed stands at about three, so it takes pretty advanced gymnastics to get between the wall and the bed and then under the doona without whacking your head on the ceiling. After several glasses of wine at dinner, our slightly impaired spatial awareness is making things worse.

Eventually, though, we manage to get in and comfortable. Then I remark that it's just as well we don't suffer from claustrophobia. A bit more thinking, and "Oh God darling, this is actually *quite* claustrophobic. We're three flights up, in a tiny attic with no hope of escape. What if there's a fire?" And that's it for me. Right here, in the middle of the night, I'm having a panic attack. The sweating starts, there are heart palpitations and I'm thinking "I have to get out of here". After ten minutes of Wendy practicing her best relaxation techniques on me, followed by the threat of a sharp slap, I calm down enough to lie back in bed. Soon, I'm snoring.

# Trouble and strife

Today we're up early for our trek to Wotton-under-Edge, which involves a 7.5-mile trek and about as much climbing as descending, both around 840 feet. Our guidebook tells us it also involves numerous criss-crossing tracks that are convoluted and confusing. So what's new? In no time at all, however, we have left the town behind and are already deep in the woods. This always baffled me about England – how suddenly, in a very short distance, you are out of a city's or town's urban build-up and smack in the middle of rural paradise. One report on the protection of rural England, says this is called the *proximity principle.* The authors claim it's the best strategy for social, economic and environmental outcomes because it allows people to use closer services, travel less, and consume less energy. I would suggest such proximity also generates greater emotional wellbeing, as residents of these cities and towns can look out of their windows to fields, trees and sheep instead of brick walls and factories.

I've tried doing a little research on *why* English towns and cities are so compact. Although there's lots of information on places that *are*, there is very little out there on *why*. So, my guess is that the reasons reach back into the country's earliest Neolithic times, when previously nomadic tribes at last began to settle and farm for a living, building permanent huts and developing a crude type of interdependence. As with many rural areas throughout Europe, the earliest villages comprised a small collection of huts that were built closely together for greater protection from both animals and other tribes. Isolation in the middle and late Neolithic period was not an attractive option for any settler, so huts were built in semi or full circles with the attendant fields surrounding them.

Later on, in the Roman and early medieval period, villages and newly created towns held to this principle. If anything, attacks and regular raids from outsiders were even more intense, so they tended to build thick, stone walls around their settlements. For this to be achievable, villages and towns needed to remain relatively compact. But again, their huts remain *inside* the walls with their fields *outside*, hence the developing proximity of rural fields to urban areas. I would suspect that as most English settlements are old, dating back centuries, if not millennia, the pattern of settlement has not changed drastically for them.

Anyway, that's the best I can come up with and I'm sticking with it.

This historic factor does make the average town much more attractive than it might otherwise have been. Urban centres back home sprawl for many miles through more or less populated areas, creating untidy, high impact environments which require you to travel some distance before you can escape. And often, by the time you leave the sprawl of one city you are already entering the next. It detracts from any aesthetic pleasure you might hope for. Here in the UK, I have found to my delight that you can move rapidly from urban to rural with minimal effort. A few minutes from your door in the centre of town will find you rambling along rural pathways, through woods, across fields, alongside lakes, taking in all that your country landscape has to offer.

Right now, we continue to climb up the surprisingly steep Stinchcombe Hill, then through broad, open fields of chest-high crops and giant English oaks. Large manor houses look out over their fine estates, with sheep wandering from one bountiful paddock to the next. Then it's into North Nibley. It is noon and not a soul's to be seen, no cars, no pedestrians, no twitching curtains, nothing to disturb the senses. The main street, the only street of the village, is unimaginatively named "The Street". Apart from the sign, there's not a lot to see. It didn't even make it into the Domesday Book, the only reference being North Knoll, the hill upon which the Tyndale monument is erected. North Nibley *does* boast a shop, run on a voluntary basis by the locals, and it claims to have a post office but we couldn't find it. There's a pub – the Black Horse Inn - and once a year the village hosts the North Nibley music festival. For the other eleven and half months, however, the place is pretty much as we find it today. We walk along "The Street" and out the other side of town and but for the sign and our trusty guidebook, we would be none the wiser about either having entered or left an inhabited settlement.

Ten minutes out of this strange town we spot the tall, narrow, stone tower of Tyndale Monument perched impressively on the hill ahead. This celebrates the life of the great William Tynsdale, who first translated the New Testament into English, and what a wonderful job he did. He was the first to create a succinct, clear interpretation for a newly literate audience and for better or worse, ensured the rapid spread of Christianity. Unfortunately, it also ensured his death at the stake.

Another woodland rises up ahead, dense and deep. After some distance we emerge and the trail now consists of white stones and rubble as it heads downhill. In a short time, the woods fade away again, and our trail leads to a small footbridge which sits at the entrance to a large, well-manicured parkland and its grand manor house. I cannot help but wonder at the sheer number of splendidly imposing estates that populate this fair region. One always seems to grace the next horizon, with their grounds ranging between large and vast. From here, we hug the top of a long plateau, climb in and out of delightful "kissing gates" and enter fields of maize that stand taller than both of us. The colours continue to beguile with their complementary hues of yellow, green, the blue of wildflowers, and the deep brown greens of woodlands. We leave the crops and enter an open field bordered by a free-flowing stream and its large, glass-like pond. The beauty almost exhausts you.

We pass yet another manor house, follow a hedgerow, turn into and emerge from woodlands and are confronted by a dense ring of conifers that close in around a strange, circular, stone wall. I would say it's forty feet in diameter and was obviously situated to take full advantage of the impressive views from the hill. The enclosure, we later discover, was built in 1815 to honour the battle of Waterloo. It's a fitting monument when you understand the context and adds to the relentless interest of this walk. The path now descends directly downhill, as it has done quite a bit this afternoon. The loss of altitude is denying us our magical views of the morning, but bringing welcome relief to over-tired muscles.

After less than ten miles, including fields, woods and a village that refused to be noticed, the town of Wotton-under-Edge comes into view. It's a lively town, boasting numerous small shops, three pubs, a supermarket and a variety of restaurants, one of which we never want to set eyes on again. By this stage in the walk the tiredness is beginning to compound. Aches and pains are common, muscles complain on a regular basis and thirst is constant. It's no surprise that our final resting point each day includes the mandatory pub. Today is no different. We head straight for the Royal Oak Inn and front up to the bar asking for our now familiar local brew. Two large pints are drawn accompanied by two bags of crisps and all is good for the next hour. It's a lovely old, traditional, English pub. No gentrification, no gastro menu, just the pub as it's been for the last couple of hundred years. Inside is brick and stone to match the exterior, with plain, small wooden tables and original chairs. A threadbare rug is the centrepiece of the room and above, low, beamed ceilings. It has a well-loved, cosy feel and appears full of regulars.

Resting our weary backsides on a couple of seats, we take long drafts from our pints and notice an elderly, grey-haired couple two tables away nodding in our direction and passing comment to each other. They look to be in their late seventies. They have friendly faces, hers bright and interested, his with that dreamy, slightly bored look. After several minutes of glancing in our direction with tentative smiles, the woman stands and makes her way towards us. Immediately she excuses herself for being so forward. She couldn't help overhearing us and wondered if we might be Australian. When we confirm her suspicions she quickly waves her husband over and asks if we would mind a chat. Without any real choice in the matter we smile and ask them to sit with us.

Edith (our new friend's name) quickly plonks herself on a chair, pulls her hesitant husband down beside her (he apologising repeatedly for the intrusion) and launches into questions about Australia and what we are "doing so far from home". She wants to know everything. How many children we have, how long we're here, what we do when back home and finally comments on how happy we look together. She is possibly the friendliest woman I have met, and interested. Before we know it, we find ourselves volunteering more information than we expected or wanted. Somehow, the woman just lulls us into a strange familiarity in which we willingly divulge our life history.

Then it's her turn. She tells us the sweetest story of how the two of them met in this same pub fifty-six years ago today. How she made eyes at him from across the room and sheepishly wandered over to ask if he'd like to join her. That was it for both of them, although his silence suggests his role in their courting was minimal. Since then, they have made a point of coming back every anniversary for just one or two drinks and to reminisce about that fateful meeting. We spend a wonderful hour with them before they wish us well and leave to drive home.

Wotton is a market town, larger than many of the settlements we have travelled through. Like them all, however, it has history by the bucket load. First mentioned in AD 940, it was where King Solomon of Wessex leased a substantial parcel of land. The town derived its name a bit later, as many towns did, simply from its location, as a woodland settlement under the edge of the hill. As with a number of places along this trail, the town also has its own ghost story, although with somewhat lusty overtones. Rumour has it that one of Wotton's more ancient houses keeps its owner awake most nights, with visits from not one, but two amorous ghosts – incubus and succubus. Just what he and these two ghosts get up to is never really divulged, and something I would rather not dwell on. But there are plenty of people in the town who enthusiastically confirm his story. Maybe they also hope for a visit one night.

Of more interest to me, are the numerous deep ditches that form rows along the periphery of town. History tells us that they were once part of a hillfort built two thousand years ago to protect the early settlement from invading tribes and later, unsuccessfully, the Romans. The settlement dates back even further than that, however, to the mid-Neolithic period. If you take your time and pay attention, you can still see remains of long and round barrows originally constructed on the edge of the current town. Like many in this land, these residents only have to step outside their homes and wander the roads to meet their most distant ancestors. Just wonderful.

# Dreaded curry and sheep

Wonderful, however, is not a term I would apply to this evening's eating experience. We check into the Swan Hotel for the night, one of our few pub accommodations. It dates to the late 1500s and creaks under the weight of its many and eventful years. Full of character, with long corridors, randomly numbered rooms, endless flights of steps and numerous anterooms, our own room is finally located on the third floor. Although in need of a facelift, it is spacious and comfortable. A quick shower, change of clothes and a search for dinner leads along the High Street. By this stage, both of us are getting a little tired of pub food. Our last Thai restaurant experience has also left us a bit cold, and the local Chinese looks forbiddingly empty. So, after some debate, it's agreed that an Indian curry is the most tempting option. Why we think so is a question that will haunt us for some days and one my stomach will remember for many more. The place looks pleasant enough, small but cosy, nice décor and happy enough looking diners. The waiters are attentive and almost too polite. Perhaps they know something we don't.

After the first course it's clear that looks can be and often are deceiving. The food is swimming in all its oily drabness. It's tasteless, devoid of any actual curry and even the waiter seems reluctant to serve it. We wash the dismal remains down with several glasses of insipid red wine and are confronted with a surprisingly expensive bill. Feeling completely uninspired and just a bit cheated, Wendy and I agree to cut our losses and get an early night.

Next morning, we're both feeling squeamish so order a light breakfast, check out of the hotel and head down the high street. From the end of the street we will again pick up the Cotswold Trail for our next destination – Hawkesbury Upton. By the time we reach the town centre, less than a mile from the hotel, Wendy is giving me an embarrassed look and is turning an unnerving shade of grey. I ask what the problem is, to which she responds, "Hold my backpack, I have to get back to the hotel" and beats a hasty retreat. I understand immediately. My poor wife. This is *not* what you need on a long day's walk. My stomach is OK so far. I figure I'll have half an hour or so to kill, so amuse myself in the local Co-op. Eventually, she resurfaces, looking a lot pinker in the face and not nearly so panicked. Her only words: "Wow, that was a close call". I thought it best not to pursue the matter.

Under the misguided impression that all is well, I lead the way to the trail at the end of town. The beginning of this day's walk could not be more picturesque. The sun is back, the sky clear and a slight, northerly breeze make for perfect conditions. Added to this is the gorgeous scenery, with deep, green woods closely bordering the path, a pretty stream running alongside us and the remains of long, cultivated terraces on each side. These are the remains of medieval farming methods, or what are called *ridge and furrow* systems. They were designed for the large, open fields of the region's manorial estate, where the Lord of the Manor owned and usually leased out his fields. Peasants, or *villeins,* worked these fields, with each row or two being rented by individual families, more if they were particularly successful. Much in the same style as a community garden or *plot* today, but as a livelihood, not a hobby. When this method ceased to operate the fields were simply turned over to grazing, and thus, the ridges remained exceptionally well preserved.

A short, steep climb brings us up to a plateau overlooking what seems to be the whole of Gloucestershire, a view that takes your breath away. Luxurious fields below melt into surrounding hills and dense woodlands before opening up again into wide vistas beyond. It's a gentle, romantic landscape that becomes almost meditative as you move through it.

## Dreams

Abruptly coming into view on our left is the majestic stonework and manicured Tudor grounds of Newark Park. In total, this masterpiece sits on just over seven hundred acres and is now owned and controlled by the National Trust. But it was originally a Tudor hunting lodge, for this area is the home of the partridge, one of Britain's most sought after and tormented birds. The fact that a lodge could later be converted to a Manor House gives some indication of just how extravagant the Tudors were. The House has welcomed and dismissed a number of wealthy owners since Tudor times, variously representing their main residence, their country escape or just their latest plaything to show off to friends and associates. Today, it serves the general public who come to imagine grander times, a more genteel England and to walk among its grounds and marvel at its architecture.

The path leading away from the house is again covered with the white flowers of wild garlic and the blues, lilacs and purples of wood violets and primroses. It's a fitting sight for such a spectacular residence. The carpet of colour opens out into broad fields of grazing sheep with their newborn in tow, crying relentlessly for their mother's milk. In no time at all we're upon the exquisite hamlet of Alderley, hopelessly pretty with the traditional Cotswold architecture and honey-coloured, sun-seeking stone cottages and grand Elms lining the pavements.

There is the old grain mill – Kilcott Mill – which dates back to the 1050s. Close by is an Elizabethan Mansion and its rows of modest cottages that housed the textile workers of the 17th and 18th centuries. On the quiet, narrow roads leading from both sides of the hamlet are magnificent arches of oak and maple trees, ushering visitors quietly into and out of this little paradise. It's a hamlet that blends dreamlike into its surrounding environment, with no harsh adjustments to perception, just the uninterrupted flow of hills and fields and harmonised village life. Wendy turns to me with bright, watery eyes and echoes my thoughts exactly, "I have never seen anything so beautiful", she whispers. What's more surprising is how a place as soothing and romantic as Alderley is not swamped with tourists. There are no buses pulling up, no tacky tourist shops selling ornaments no-one really wants, no tourist centres. There is just the quiet solitude of a hamlet content with its own setting and way of life, as it probably has been for the past thousand years. We have a strong desire to remain here as long as possible, to at least briefly, belong in this exceptional place.

*And it starts*

But alas, we can't. It's time to leave this dream where it sits, comfortably and permanently in the Cotswold dales. Heading off along the trail once more for the last leg to Hawkesbury Upton, I feel an ominous 'ping' in my stomach, then a gurgle. I quickly search for somewhere secluded off the track. Fortunately, we routinely pack a roll of toilet paper in the backpack, in case of emergency. Right here and now is one of those times. I decide there is nothing for it but to climb over the nearby dry-stone wall to find cover in a field. The field, of course, belongs to a farm and the farmhouse is at the bottom of the hill, but I judge it too far away to be a real deterrent.

Let's just say I get down to business in rapid fashion. But squatting down as I am, in this open field, I begin to feel I'm being watched. Turning slowly around I'm startled to see a dozen curious sheep no more than ten feet away, gathered in a semi-circle staring at me. They are extremely unnerving. It's time to leave, and quickly. By the time I leap back over the stone wall, Wendy is laughing uncontrollably. From her vantage point I can see the humour.

Another three miles on and the sign for Hawkesbury Upton comes into view. It has been a long and eventful day, some of the events we would rather forget, and I'll have nightmares about sheep for some time yet. But we have arrived at last. Even the slightly off-putting sign as you enter town, proclaiming that: "You'll never leave", fails to dampen our spirits.

# The splendour of escape

Hawkesbury Upton is listed as a large village with 1,200 souls. Unusually for a village this size, it only has two pubs. Both sit on the High Street. One of these, the Fox Inn, and fortunately, the nicer looking, is where we're staying tonight. This village strikes me as somehow not quite right. Sure, it is as pretty as many other Cotswold villages, though not as beautiful as some. Although a decent size, it has a *small* feel to it. It's friendly, boasts the traditional Cotswold architecture, albeit, with some new, less traditional amendments, and the pubs have their usual gathering of locals sitting quietly over their pints of ale. There is a mandatory stream running through the centre of the village, with Willows overhanging and manicured cottage gardens full of Daffodils, Freesias and Grape Hyacinths.

But there is something else here. I think that if I had a little more imagination, I could create a rather dark crime thriller about this village, a story in which everything seemed sweet and above board on the surface, but which hid some dark secrets. I am almost certainly doing this village a great disservice, and I have nothing but good to say for our experience here. Perhaps it's the fact that the residents here seem to know each other *too* well, or that the village as a whole is a little too neat and tidy and well-tended. It reminds me of the American movie "The Truman Show". The village and its people appear somehow scripted.

After checking in to the hotel it's time for a leisurely stroll around the few available streets. You may think this is a bit strange after a nine-mile walk, and it probably is, but walking such distances each day kind of gets under your skin. Over time, it becomes difficult to stop. You become addicted to moving. So, we were moving through this pretty and somewhat unsettling village, smiling and nodding at the few local inhabitants walking their dogs. One woman in particular wants to stop and talk and we both dutifully pat her Corgi, which brings a smile to her face. She leans across and places her hand on Wendy's shoulder. "Where are you from love?" and then relays stories of all the friends, relatives and other assorted folk who had ever lived, visited, or intend to visit Australia. She explains how she had once visited Western Australia when she was young and ended up staying for a year. She would love to return but can't encourage her "lazy so-and-so of a husband" to leave the Cotswolds. The woman is extremely friendly, and in my new conspiratorial mood, I think perhaps a bit too friendly.

Turning left and left again will hopefully bring us back to the Fox Inn for an anticipated Italian feast at their award-winning restaurant. I lead us into a side-street that boasts large stone houses with manicured gardens, arched rose walkways and invisible occupants. Up on the left is a fine house with a three-foot high stone wall encircling the yard. Suddenly, Wendy calls out an "Oh, how cute!" and leans against the wall to pat a "sweet" puppy. The only visible part of this "puppy" is its head, resting on the top-most stone of the wall. As she reaches over, the so-called puppy turns into a rather large and irritable Doberman. It leaps at her, barking viciously and almost taking her hand off. Wendy springs back and turns in a single, adrenalin-fuelled movement, then sprints past me looking deathly pale. When I finally catch up with my trembling partner, she suggests (between numerous expletives) that we end our stroll immediately.

The problem is that we have a small, three-year-old, brown and white fluff-ball at home that is officially known as a Cavoodle. It is timid, loving and wouldn't know how to go about biting someone. She trembles when strangers approach or other dogs look at her. Wendy automatically thinks all dogs should be the same. To her horror and near misses over the years, she's found that many aren't.

There was a raucous night ahead at the Fox Inn with fellow walkers. I'm not sure where these walkers come from. Rarely do we come across them on the trail, or even in the pubs and shops along the way. Yet randomly, a bunch of them will appear in the same village as us come nightfall. We begin with a delicious Italian meal of pasta (Gluten free for me), meatballs, Ossobuco, pizza and some heavenly Italian wine. We finish with a pint too many of the pub's best bitter. The gaggle of walkers, us included, then drift off to our respective beds with slurred farewells. Apparently, I snored thunderously all night, an accusation of Wendy's which was confirmed all too enthusiastically by the woman in the next room. Our breakfast, therefore, was eaten largely in silence, before filling day-packs and once again stepping into a chill morning for another long day of tramping.

*Onward to Tormarton*

Two miles of walking through, I must say, almost unnaturally beautiful surroundings, and Wendy, picks her moment. She sidles alongside me, links her arm through mine, and says in a meek voice, that she's possibly miscalculated. "Miscalculated what?", I ask, remembering Wendy's curious dyslexia. So, it came as no surprise that she had had a problem calculating the number of walking days for our trip. I have to admit that this walk has been one of the best experiences of my life and, after a short break, I would do it again in a heart-beat. By this stage, however, the weariness was hitting us. Each and every day we are walking long distances, up some very steep hills, along woodland tracks, and regularly becoming lost.

When she said she had miscalculated the days, for a fleeting moment I thought that maybe, just maybe, we only had two days left instead of three. But no, she had counted too few, and it now seems we have four more days of tired bones, sore feet, and aching back muscles. Wendy explains all this whilst massaging my shoulders and being at her loving best. I just respond by giving her the most withering look I can muster, turn back to the track and march on silently. But secretly, I didn't mind too much. Although we are weary beyond doubt, it does mean we get to spend another day in these glorious surroundings and this most liberating freedom from care.

One of the most profound blessings of this trip, and one I heartily recommend be taken up by any and all middle-aged couples, is the opportunity to escape. Escape your everyday monotony of daily rituals and routines, your house and its upkeep, and mind-numbing domesticity. It is wonderfully emancipating to escape to an idyllic spot such as this and walk for days on end unhindered and unencumbered, through the most sublime countryside. To meet locals who want to talk, to experience, if only briefly, their unique ways of life and their cherished villages. To understand that there is a whole world outside your own little bubble that is in urgent need of exploring and appreciating. This is what travelling means, *experiencing* rather than simply *looking*.

This walk has provided the best gift of all. The therapy of walking in nature, in sunshine, without people and expectations crowding in upon you, cannot be overstated. Cares melt away. The lines in our faces soften. Tension disappears. We laugh at each other, and together, are closer and more content. We shrug off inconveniences, take joy in the simplest things, things we would not normally have even noticed. Here is the taste of another, better, more rewarding life.

Today, this life is leading us to Tormarton, and, for once, we are losing altitude over the day. The guidebook tells us that there are only 476 feet of ascent but 590 feet of descent. At this stage of the walk, both of us get excited about anything that points downhill instead of interminable climbs. The blue skies that have bathed us in sunshine and warmth for the previous ten days have finally vanished, with a fine drizzle starting early. Already, we are in our wet weather gear, with rain jackets, waterproof pants, and hoods. But the mood isn't sombre. Entering another dense woodland, with rain dripping softly from leaves and a light mist rising across a stream it feels uncannily like a scene from *Wind in the Willows.* There is a wistfulness in the air, a quiet loosening of the spirit.

Eventually returning to reality, it's time to consult our guidebook again. Increasingly it has become a substitute for the absence of trail markers at critical times. Only this time, it suggests we follow the hedge running along the edge of the field for one mile. There *is* no hedge. To make matters worse, the track soon divides into five separate, vague paths, two of which fade after a hundred yards or so. The others lead off in radically different directions. Wendy heads off to investigate and soon returns with a smile on her face and news she has found a Cotswold marker.

Between track markers and guide books you can *almost* navigate this trail. Expect to get lost at least once a day and if you're unfortunate enough to share our navigation skills, perhaps several more times.

At last we're out of the woods and into open fields again, the view opening up to show us a grand, grey stone mansion in manicured grounds at the bottom of the hill. Even though the manor is in a shallow valley, shrouded in Beech and Elm trees, the sunlight hits the stone of the house and illuminates the entire structure. Parts of this manorial estate – Horton Court - were constructed in the 12th century. Like many, it is now owned by the National Trust, allowing the public to share in its noble history. It was once a Norman Hall and since that time, has witnessed hundreds of years of conquest, settlement, and royal claims. The original builder and inhabitant happened to be a kinsman of William the Conqueror's innermost party. The property was a reward for his loyalty and service. This generous donation also ensured its regal legacy. Its prominence continued into the early Tudor period, its owner dealing directly with Pope Clement in the hope of securing the annulment of Henry VIII's marriage to Katherine of Aragon.

Before this more recent history, however, the actual spot upon which Horton Court was built was at the centre of a pretty significant Iron-Age settlement, complete with hill forts, farming enclosures and sacred religious meeting places. History carried it forward from here to a period of Roman occupation, where it became an administrative hive of bureaucracy. To cap it all off, the Manor finally received recognition and gravitas as England's oldest occupied house. It is important to understand just how significant this place is as one of England's most historically and politically decisive monuments. Regardless of its role in the country's events over the last several thousand years, it is in itself a most charming house and remains a drawcard for tourist and historians alike.

## Sod Off

The next punctuation in our walk is the infinitesimal hamlet of Little Sodbury. This minute settlement is one of a triumvirate, with sisters Old Sodbury and Chipping Sodbury close by. Old Sodbury is a little larger, making the grade as *village*. It's every bit as old as Little Sodbury. Beginning life 2,500 years ago, it later becomes home to the Roman army and later again the Saxons, who used the remnants of the old fort for their own stronghold in the late 6th century. As did many of these little villages, the three Sodbury's featured in William's Domesday Book. The magnificent church here is the Church of St John the Baptist, another Norman construction which first opened in 1240. Old Sodbury is a vibrant village with strong community spirit. Newsletters, 'Village Open Days', a school, library, football club and church groups are all thriving. But, like many small settlements it's unfortunately in focus for possible housing development. If managed correctly, this may well add to the village's vitality, but track records of such developments do not provide optimism.

Currently, though, the village retains an intimate feel and spirit. The community newsletter spends a column welcoming a couple and their two small children just moving into the village. There are advertisements for lunch time concerts at the school. There's a notice about how the "short mat bowls club" is faring in its current competition, as well as a reminder about adult classes in domestic cooking. Most prominent, is the Old Sodbury Women's Institute (WI), which is in the midst of celebrating its 99th birthday.

And what an amazing organisation it is. First formed in 1915 to help regenerate rural villages and communities as well as encouraging women to produce much needed essentials during the First World War, it has since grown enormously. Now it involves itself in everything from providing rural women with education opportunities, healthcare, employment, and skill development, as well as being very active in campaigns that will rescue and rejuvenate the community spirit. Currently, it has more than 220,000 members spread across 6,000 WI subsidiaries. They must be doing something right, because it ranks as one of the most successful and powerful associations in the country, one that can bring politicians to their knees if it so chooses.

Chipping Sodbury is the largest of all three settlements. It's classified as a market town with a population of around five thousand. This is several times larger than Old Sodbury and many times larger than Little Sodbury. Apart from that claim to fame, Chipping Sodbury oddly boasts the second widest street in the whole of England. Apparently, when it was constructed room was made for a host of animal pens to supply the local agricultural markets.

Of more interest, it's the birth place of JK Rowling, the author of the most famous Harry Potter series. Born in this picturesque town fifty-three years ago at the Chipping Sodbury Maternity Hospital, she spent the first nine years of her life roaming the charming Cotswold countryside. It was here that she gained early inspiration for some of her famous literary characters. Harry, she claims, was drawn from a mischievous school friend by the name of Ian Potter, whose humorous capers and childhood pranks provided plenty of ideas for her central character. The irritable and unreasonable Aunt Marge was based to a large extent on her very own maternal grandmother, a woman who unsettled her as a child and obviously gave her cause to reflect in less than charitable ways. And the creepy, if ultimately noble Professor Snape was drawn from one of her less popular teachers, whose name she has kindly refused to divulge.

Early signs of Rowling's talent emerged when she was six. Indulging her imaginative bent, JK wrote a book about a rabbit that had measles, which her mother praised with enthusiasm until the child began nagging to get it published. If only her mother had known (or perhaps she had) of the enormous talent and imagination that her child would one day bring to the world of book lovers and marketing gurus alike. From the humblest of beginnings great things sometimes arise.

For the crime followers among you, the murder of a Chipping Sodbury student on Christmas Day in 1997 led to another spectacular achievement, although not as enjoyable or innocent. In an attempt to catch the murderer, police insisted that more than 4,500 men give samples of their bodily fluids to either be eliminated from their enquiries, or placed squarely in the spotlight as chief suspect. In the largest DNA test to date, British police paved the way for the first nation-wide DNA database that is nowadays both familiar and frightening. The database came into existence quickly indeed. You see, local and then national politicians caught wind of what was going on and realised the political mileage they could make from such a dramatic crime.

Tantalisingly, the crime was committed on Christmas Day; it involved the murder of a female teenager, who was naked when found, and the press were wholly enraptured with the case's salacious nature. Politicians had to be seen to commit themselves to protecting young people from scourges such as this. In addition, DNA testing was a very sexy new technology that made for compelling slogans and parliamentary speeches. It was rushed through the House of Commons and Lords in record time with many patting themselves on the back for bringing in such a commendable law. And along with the miracle that became JK Rowling, it very much put Chipping Sodbury on all kinds of maps.

# Bright lights, big city?

We were rather chuffed when realising that the next mile of our walk took us right through the middle of the Dog Inn. It's still drizzling, so there's no reason *not* to take advantage of this fortuitous obstacle and grab a quick pint. The Dog Inn is over five hundred years old, and looks it. It advertises itself as providing the ambience of a traditional English pub. There is a heavy oak entrance door, low, solid oak beams, and dense English Ivy growing over the front wall. I open the door into a large bar room where the dozen or so tables are empty. Instead, the customers, who incidentally are all male, are crowded around the small bar. There must be fifteen or so of them.

Wendy and I help ourselves to the choice of tables before I make my way to the bar. And that's when I understand why the bar is so crowded. Serving these gentlemen is a young, attractive barmaid who has decided to accentuate her curves with some rather snug fitting clothes. The men are largely ignoring each other and keenly vying for the barmaid's attention. Corny jokes are being told, laughter is overly loud and eye contact is firmly where it shouldn't be. You can tell that the young woman is used to such attention and expects me to join the others in their fascination. With Wendy's eyes now following the scene, however, I become overly self-righteous and focus somewhere over the barmaid's left shoulder while I order.

From here, it's only a stone's throw to the excitingly large and thriving city of Bristol. Well, it's more like seventeen miles, but out here in the solitude of the Cotswolds, that's close enough. Bristol is home to half a million souls which is roughly 3,600 times the population of Little Sodbury. Depending on your ancient etymology, you might like to call Bristol *Caer Odor, Bric, Bricstow,* or *Brycgstow,* depending on whether you prefer Welsh, Celtic, Saxon, or old English. It can match any other town, village or city in terms of history. It can also mix it with the best of them in terms of Neanderthal remnants, hill forts, Roman villas, or Norman castles. But the city has a darker history as well, claiming more than its fair share of the 18th and 19th century English slave trade. More than 500,000 wretched African souls were shipped to the Americas from Bristol Harbour, never to see their homeland again or know that sweet taste of freedom.

After the demise of the Royal African Company, Bristol's first slave ship was perversely named the *Beginning*. It certainly wasn't the beginning for the victims of this depraved trade, but very much the *end*. It is estimated that the slave ships from Bristol alone numbered more than two thousand, doing a roaring trade with 100% profits before public outcry, initiated in a wonderful little pub by the name of *Seven Stars*, finally curtailed their activities. These years of slave trading represent a monstrous blight on an otherwise remarkable history spanning thousands of years.

Modern Bristol is a world away from these events, being one of Britain's most cosmopolitan, diverse and pleasant cities. It's economy also remains one of the country's most resilient, being the envy of London, Manchester, Liverpool and Edinburgh. The port city generates most of its wealth from aerospace, manufacturing, agriculture, creative industries, and real estate, whilst maintaining a vibrant cultural scene and progressive education program.

More importantly, Bristol is the home of the potent and ubiquitous children's syrup – Ribena. As well, it boasts the birthplace of that most fearsome and famous of pirates, Blackbeard, who although a criminal, was not morally corrupt enough to involve himself in the transport of enslaved human beings. Perhaps the most fascinating of all, though, is Bristol's Llandoger Trow pub. It's one of the oldest pubs in the land and the local watering hole for many of Southern England's pirates, including Blackbeard. And, when originally built in 1664, it is said to have been constructed on wheels so that it could be rolled back and forwards depending on the tides. I think that could be listed as one of engineering's greatest achievements.

To many in the Cotswolds, Bristol is simply a big city on their outskirts and one that doesn't interfere too much with their way of life. We are certainly too tired to let it interfere with ours, as we count down the final miles to tonight's destination – Tormarton. The route winds through large Sycamore, Elm and London Plane trees in close company, before ploughing straight through the middle of Sodbury Camp. This, I would say, is one of the best-preserved Bronze-Age forts I have come across, with two rows of ramparts, indicating just how important it was at the time. The fort's location on a local farm has probably helped ensure its preservation; let's hope it remains this way for some generations to come.

From the fort's position high up on the hill, you can quite easily, even on a drizzly day such as today, view the majestic range of the Brecon Beacons. Although the Beacons lie in Southern Wales, their height of almost 3,000 feet in some places, guarantees their visibility for many miles. They intersperse regularly with deep valleys that go by unpronounceable names such as Cwm Sere, Cwm Cynwyn, Cwn Oergwm, and Cwm Cwareli. There is a legend in these parts, that near the glacial lake between two valleys, there is a secret doorway camouflaged within a rock (Moria again comes to mind). It opens each May Day (a *politically motivated* rock) and allows one to enter a passage leading through to an island. Along this passage a great number of fairies gather to entertain themselves and any open-minded (or perhaps asylum escapee) visitor who cares to join them. The area is also visited quite a lot around Christmas, as one of the villages goes by the name of Bethlehem. Visitors flock here to buy and send Christmas cards with the Bethlehem postmark.

# Farms, churches, and food

Entering Tormarton is a seductive experience. You cross a large meadow of wildflowers scattered amongst dense carpets of greenest grass. These are punctuated by a large, mirrored pond complete with bulrushes and dancing dragonflies, followed by a ring of beautiful stone houses around the perimeter of the village. It's like a landscape painting suddenly come to life. Tormarton is a village of working farms, and is therefore, bustling with the usual type of farm life. A tractor is trundling down a side street towing a cart of baled hay, there is a farm equipment shop on the high street, two wholesale produce stores side by side, and large flocks of Cotswold sheep grazing in surrounding fields. There is a tangibly earthy feel to this village.

On the left is the St Mary Magdalene Church - an imposing grey stone building which is currently Grade 1 listed, and dates back to before the Norman Invasion. Originally, the Church was listed as "Saxon", suggesting it is quite a bit older than some have claimed. A stroll through the adjoining cemetery reveals headstones that date to the 1600s. Granted, you have to rub the lettering and numbers to clear some of the moss away, but there they are, revealing the deaths, many quite young, of our four-hundred-year-old ancestors. If you venture into the church itself, you travel even further back in time. Here, you come across black marble tombs of Sir John de la Rivere, buried 1350 and Sir John Sendlow, buried 1493.

Along with many villages and towns in this area of Outstanding Natural Beauty, settlement around Tormarton began roughly six thousand years ago. In fact, *Tormartons* will proudly tell you that unlike many of their neighbours, six ancient skeletons uncovered in the late twentieth century provide all the evidence required to demonstrate their little village was already in full swing by the middle of the Bronze Age. They will claim to have confirmation of a thriving Neolithic community of productive farms, large herds and regular religious rituals. The village then travelled through the usual path of Roman, Norman, and Saxon settlement with even a quick though unsustainable flirtation with a few errant Vikings. Today, Tormarton is very much a small but thriving settlement with a little less than 350 souls. It has had its time in the lime-light. There was a fairly constant stream of aristocrats and royals between the late Saxon and late medieval period, the last in that long line being the Duke of Beaufort, occupying the current Manor House.

As Australians, the only connection we have with Tormarton, is one dating from the 1820s. An unfortunate young labourer and resident of the village – Joseph Pike – was found guilty of breaking into neighbours' houses and sentenced to transportation for fourteen years in our penal colony - Sydney Cove. After his time was served, he was granted a *ticket of leave* – a title which meant you were free but being watched closely. If you so much as looked sideways, you'd be doing time again. He took his leave seriously enough, though, and went on to marry a female convict who had just received her own *ticket*. Together, they moved to a small, barely settled town called Dapto, where he and his new bride established a farm. He farmed productively, made some money on wheeling and dealing in farm equipment and stock and with this new prosperity in hand, the couple then moved to the seaside town of Kiama, several miles away. After some years and enough time for most to have forgotten his previous lifestyle, Pike set up the town's first shop, became a Councilman, and one of Kiama's leading citizens. He also found time to have ten children by his long-suffering wife. Interestingly for us, it just so happens that the towns of Dapto and Kiama are a mere stone's throw from our own home in Australia, and places we know well. Now that *is* a connection to savour.

By now, we have traversed this very appealing village and our hotel is coming into view. It's a Compass Inn, a motel really, and the only accommodation in the village. Lugging our backpacks and three bags of shopping up the drive the incessant drizzle finally slows to a stop, just as shelter is available. We book in and head to our room, which is immaculately clean, comfortable, warm and small.

Our night on the edge of this small village, in a conventional chain motel turns out to be surprisingly good. Since it's the only one for a couple of miles in any direction we decide on the motel restaurant, always a gamble. But it's superb. The waitresses obviously know their trade. The ambience is friendly and relaxed, and the meals have been sourced from local ingredients and are delicious. Apparently, they get quite a bit of custom from the nearby market town of Chippenham, about 12 miles to the east, so the restaurant procured itself an award-winning chef to meet the demand. The staff even let us bring our own bottle of wine to drink, which I'd been hanging onto for the past couple of days. We retire late to our room after the nicest meal we have had in some time, a bottle of Bordeaux and one, maybe two whiskeys to remove the final aches and pains.

Morning breaks and it's time to leave the lovely farming community of Tormarton. The weather outside is not at all inviting. It's dark, brooding, squally, with sudden gusts of cold, wet wind. Rain is steady and it doesn't look like letting up anytime soon. All-in-all, pretty miserable. Yet go out we must. Three layers of clothing, damp walking shoes back on, laden backpacks hitched, waterproof pants and rain jackets sealed, another quick coffee to insulate us a bit more. Then, after a chuckle as we realise we look more like arctic explorers than mere Cotswold wanderers, it's out the door and along the path.

The trail winds its way through the remainder of the village, appearing to take every road available. Finally, it straightens itself out and leads off across a small bridge that has seen better days. Broad grass banks line each side of the road with wild garlic growing on one side and a high, dry-stone wall on the other. The cottages on this side of town are even more attractive than those within the village proper. They are large, of the Cotswold stone, sit in exquisitely manicured gardens and blend seamlessly into their surroundings. Our guidebook tells us to make our way between the last of these two houses and turn left at the shed beyond. Such quaint directions in such congested times are a welcome anomaly. When towns and cities are crowded with domestic, commercial and industrial buildings all on top of each other and one looking very much like the other, the Cotswolds must be one of the few places left where a guidebook can confidently tell you to *"turn left at the shed"* and for the shed to be there, alone and obvious.

Around the shed we go, already feeling the effects of a biting wind and a steady soaking. The landscape from here on is quite different to the rest of the walk. Opening out in front of us are large, flat, open fields that stretch for miles at a time. No longer are there the small fields bordered with hedges and wildflowers that we have become so used to. This is the land of agribusiness now, not the individual farmer. Giant machines plough fields, sow crops and spread fertiliser, feeding the supermarkets of Britain and to a large extent, Europe. And believe me, it is *big* business. Last year alone, land under agriculture in the UK increased by another 0.7% to cover 72% of all available land. The industry employs over 470,000 people and contributes about $8.5 billion to the economy. Wheat, rapeseed oil, sugar beet, various fruits, beef, veal, mutton, lamb, pork, and poultry remain the largest products. Unfortunately, however, organic methods and applications remain depressingly low. In Britain's agribusiness hubs you don't see the hand harvesting or sowing or organic fertilising, or single plough grading, owner-occupier approach that can be witnessed throughout much of the Cotswold area. And here we are right on the edge of such vastness. Luckily, we will be skirting around much of it, remaining for most of the time, safely within the "natural zone".

Our trail winds its way along the edge of the remarkable Dyrham Park, a showpiece of Tudor architecture. The Manor sits grandly at the end of a long gravel path bordered on each side by wide strips of manicured lawn and large beds of the most luxurious and colourful plants. I imagine it takes quite a number of full-time gardeners all day, every day to maintain such perfection. The gravel path directs your eye to the very centre of the Manor House, sitting astride its vast property in all its majesty. Originally, the house was built for William Blathwayt who happened to be Secretary of State for King William III in the 1690s. Which just goes to show how well these "hangers-on" were paid for their ducking and bowing. Then, as now, the house was filled with works of the Dutch Masters, ornate furniture, gilded gold and silver, priceless antiques, as well as intricate floors and coverings. Most of the Blathwayt family remain buried in the grounds, which incidentally, cover more than 270 acres of lawn, specially designed with planted forests, lakes, ponds and grand statues. There are herds of fallow deer roaming the property, a collection of pheasants and a multitude of other wild-life. It really is a dreamscape, for which thousands hand over money to wander the grounds... and pay the gardeners.

The house, of course, represents the grand entrance to the actual hamlet of Dyrham, which delights in its idyllic setting along the River Boyd. This is a tiny place that, because of its proximity to main commuter arteries, has become more cosmopolitan in recent years. Being in close proximity to both Bath and Bristol has also helped curb the exodus of younger residents which plagues so many other rural villages. But again, like others, it has lost its school, pub, post office and shops, so that today it is a resident-only paradise. Its population prefers to travel the few miles required for supermarket prices and big city conveniences.

This wasn't always the case. In 577, Dyrham was the strategic centre of a battle for power and ultimate control. Two of the greatest Saxon leaders – Cuthwine and Ceawlin – fought it out here with the more entrenched but less forward-thinking Britons, who ended up losing three of their kings to this pair. The Saxons gradually gained control of the entire area, and then, ultimately, Britain. The village evolved and prospered until the late medieval period. It gained its own squire who ran the village in typical feudal style with economic planning effective enough for his family and at least the more notable yeomen and tenant farmers to prosper. Today, it has settled back into a sleepy settlement where city workers retire at night and weekends to live their rural dream while fretting over their second mortgages and commuter costs.

# Cold dates and Cottage Pie

The drizzle continues throughout the day, with gusty, biting winds that gnaw our bones. The scenery is also less pleasing. Open fields with few trees, no hedges, and the off brown of recently harvested crops is our only view. There is no differentiation to the landscape to catch our interest. It is with some considerable relief, then, that as we crest a final hill, Wendy announces triumphantly that the pocket-sized village in front of us is indeed, the sought-after Cold Ashton. And I must say, that in the midst of such barren landscape, it is an oasis of charm. It is nestled into the side of a hill, complete in its isolation and loveliness. Stone walls line the main street, giving an air of permanence. The architecture of the Old Rectory and the nearby courthouse cap off this nursery rhyme picture, and its tiny population of two hundred souls ensures that this setting, is to a large extent, uninterrupted.

The size of the village has diminished considerably from its heyday in the 1850s, when the famous Cotswold sheep and wool commanded the local economy and brought great prosperity. It was also once part of the great Bath Abbey Estate. Its attractiveness and prime position under the edge of the hill, however, meant that it was worth far more to the monks broken up and sold off in small parcels, than it was sitting idle within their cloistered empire. With monks being monks, there was no room for sentimentality or consideration of the estate's aesthetic beauty when there was money to be made. It was sold off quickly and at highly inflated prices, and money flowed freely into God's pantry, wine cellar and increasingly deep pockets.

If you travel back further than this mercenary episode, you find that William the Conquerer records the local population of Cold Ashton as a mere eight households, with one plough-team, six acres under agriculture and only three households making enough to be taxed. I suppose that over a thousand years you have to expect some ups and downs. Today, Cold Ashton is still relatively prosperous, having an unemployment rate of only 1.2%, comparing very favourably with the rest of Britain. It's citizens also record a favourable level of health compared to the national average, and tourism is sustained, if not hectic. You may not find a great deal of cultural diversity, as the village claims 99% of its citizens are white and about 85% of them Christian. There is one person listed as Indian and one as Asian (other), which would be OK as long as you weren't the Indian or Asian (other). The village also claims to be "safe". In the past month there was a total of one crime committed which was described as "non-urgent". Possibly an unruly tourist or defecting Christian.

It's fair to say that the village of Cold Ashton has no services, so the only thing you can expect for the night is a bed. There is one other great disappointment for us. After a day of cold and wet, the thing we wanted most was to settle into the warmth of the Plough Inn for a pint or two before heading to our accommodation. The first person we asked of its whereabouts was a newcomer to the village and didn't know. Even so, we thought it a bit strange that in a village this size you didn't know where your local was, even if you'd only arrived yesterday. The next person we came across was a local farmer who gave us a sad, sympathetic smile and relayed the tragic tale of the pub's closure a couple of years beforehand. It took us a while to accept this unwanted response.

"Are you sure?"

"Yes".

"Is there another close by?"

"No, sorry."

"How can that be? What do we do?"

These last two questions were met with an apologetic shrug. We thanked the man for his time and moved on in a desultory fashion indeed. I could not understand how the villagers weren't up in arms and storming the council offices. It's a sad state of affairs when the only village for miles decides to close its single pub.


I learn to my dismay that pub closures are becoming increasingly common here in the UK. Currently, in Britain, there are almost 53,000 pubs. In 2000, however, there were over 60,000. Last year alone, witnessed more than 1,400 closures, and in the recent past, these closures have been running at a rate of 27 per week. So far, London seems the worst hit, with a 25% reduction in pubs over the past sixteen years. Fortunately, over the last six months the rate of closures has begun to slow, now running at 18 per week, but brewery associations have warned that unless beer duties are cut further in Britain, this latest respite will be short lived. Others blame a change of drinking habits, with British increasingly preferring gin and craft beers. Some say it's the smoking ban that has caused such a dramatic drop in pub attendance. Others believe Brits are changing their entertainment destinations through fashion. Perhaps, speculate some, UK adults are just drinking less, while others still, usually those in the "batty camp", claim it's all the fault of those nasty banks that caused the 2008 GFC. Historians tell us that the British pub has been in slow decline since the 19th century and provide pretty convincing stats to back up their argument. The jury is still firmly out on exactly what the cause is, or if it *is* in fact, a combination of all the above.

Rural pubs have managed to battle longer and harder. Dr Matthew Mount conducted a study a few years back on whether or not the village pub lived up to its name and reputation. He talked to people in 284 parishes located at least five miles outside a city or large town and asked their opinions on their local. His study concluded that the village pub had "a statistically significant impact on social engagement and involvement among residents .... (and) provided opportunities for communal initiatives". Or, in plain speak, rural residents like their pubs.

But I suppose it goes some way to showing that the more isolated your community, the more you rely on your local pub for bonding, which certainly explains why they are closing so much faster in cities like London. As people move away from these small villages, and as others use them for second homes or weekend retreats, it's obvious that visits to the local are going to drop. This is a sad state of affairs, as I think you could safely say the village pub has been one of the most binding influences in its community since medieval times. In many important ways it has also helped shape the uniqueness and character of that community. They *are* the community and the community *is* them. They are critical to the very fabric that weaves these isolated people together. Thankfully, apart from Cold Ashton, Wendy and I have for our part, found the village pub to be alive and well, and we are doing our damnedest to keep it that way.

Our accommodation for tonight is among a group of small (tiny in fact) but well designed and maintained stone huts. They have been built at the rear of the owner's farm to cater specifically to Cotswold Way walkers. As these represent the only accommodation in the village and the only for some miles either way, she does a roaring trade. Tonight, however, mid-week and raining, Wendy and I are the only guests in residence. The owner had obviously been waiting for us. The moment we come through the gate she is there to meet us, apologising for the rain and promising to get us inside as soon as possible. She is courteous and efficient, nothing more, nothing less.

Gratefully, we step out of the drenching rain and into our warm, centrally heated hut. It is a strangely deceptive phenomenon that places are often much bigger when you step through the door than they appear from outside. Well, these aren't. As we enter the room we both trip over the bed and I whack my elbow on the wardrobe. A quick squeeze around the edge of the bed brings us straight into the minute bathroom. If you want to sit on the toilet you have to shrink yourself into the gap between the door and the shower recess. But it *is* tastefully decorated and very clean. For one night, it's all we need. In her efficient manner the host lets us know that there is afternoon tea waiting for us in the kitchen.

By this stage, we're both ravenous. We make quick work of squeezing out our door and hot-footing it to the guest kitchen. Because there are no services, shops, restaurants, or apparently, a pub in the village, all food is provided (for a price) on site. Wendy had called ahead to let the woman know I was "Gluten Free". So, when we front up to the table, there is a plate with two delicious looking slices of fruit loaf and a cup of tea waiting for Wendy, and a single dried date waiting for me. Perhaps I expect too much, but after a twelve mile walk in the rain, I was hoping for a bit more than a dried date. The disappointment was to continue. The owner happily informs me that for dinner she'd been able to buy a nice gluten free surprise. Later that evening, I'm delighted to see Cottage Pie written on the container's cover. Now, nothing quite gets me excited like a good, meaty cottage pie. You might then, imagine my horror when she announces that it is also *vegan*, made with chickpeas and lentils, no meat whatsoever. Not only do I steer away from vegan meals whenever possible, but for me, lentils and chickpeas, represent the devil. I detest them, and they detest me. We had also paid ahead for wine to accompany the meal, but the owner's selection was unspeakably bad. All-in-all then, a dismal end to a dismal day.

## Blind-man's Bluff

Today is our final walking day. We have woken from a warm, cosy sleep to the sound of steady rain on the roof. I suppose it was only a matter of time. Luck has smiled on us for most of this walk and I would rather have the rain at the end than at the beginning. But looking outside, there's heavy mist as well. Our record for keeping to the trail is not good, even in clear weather. Today, you can't see ten feet in front of you. I suspect it could be a longer walk than our guidebook is claiming. We set off, covered from head to toe in wet weather gear, with hoods pulled so tight that only eyes and nose are exposed. Confidence drops when we can't even find the gate out of the property. Mist is so thick that it's difficult to tell whether we're going uphill or down. Oh joy!

I'm not sure if this route has a pub or even a coffee shop on the way to recharge. It may well have, but how on earth would we know in this porridge? The other problem with fog like this is that it tends to cancel out any and all sound. There are no birds singing this morning, and the fog has cut all sound of wind, faint noises from distant villages, or the sheep and cow utterances that usually emanate from nearby paddocks. There is just silence. After a couple of hours this becomes quite eerie. Wendy studies the map closely as she walks, trying to decipher the squiggly lines on the guide's by now sodden, grey pages. She has a tough job and the frustration is beginning to show. At last she pulls her phone out to try for a GPS reading. There is none. We are in the middle of nowhere, with no reception. Just us and the wet guidebook. Eventually we stumble, quite by accident, onto a path with a post. Miraculously, it's the Cotswold trail again and its leading towards a farm.

## Frightful farmers

National trails through farms are not normally an issue. Farmers are required to keep these paths clear for walkers and maintain the kissing gates through which they pass. So far, we have passed through numerous farms and across too many private properties to count on this walk. The property owners we have come across have been polite and usually given a cheery hello or wave as we pass by. But on this particular farm the sign near the farm gate has obviously been removed, leaving a broken off post where it once stood, and the trail simply vanishes again. Wendy studies her guidebook for a clue while I walk along the fence-line looking for some sort of hint. She works out that the path has to lead from the bottom of the paddock and work its way diagonally across the field. Deciding to jump the fence, we trudge around in circles before the path suddenly appears through the fog, straight ahead. But in less than a dozen feet it has disappeared again, and not this time, because of the fog. This particularly nasty little farmer has not only broken the marker from its post. He has ploughed over the entire length of the path across his field. We walk his field in every direction for an hour. There is nothing. The path has been covered over. There are strings of curses and expletives and fantasies of what I would do to the particular farmer if I ever came across him, but it doesn't really help. Eventually, we split up and walk in opposite directions to see if the trail resurfaces. We encounter barbed wire fences, giant patches of stinging nettles and thick fog. Finally, a cry from Wendy that she's found the path. We are wet, cold and frustrated but at last heading in the right direction again.

According to the guidebook, Lansdown Hill battlefield is soon on our right and apparently, a sight to behold. But the only thing we can see is the continuing white blanket. It was here in 1643 that Sir William Waller attempted to defend the riches of Bath from the invading Royalists. He failed but he made the Royalists pay dearly for the privilege. It was Waller's four thousand troops against the Royalists' six thousand so it was never going to be pretty. Although the Royalists won the day they did think twice before doing battle with these brutal fellows again. Being English, there is now an annual celebration of the battle, and this year's promises to be "better than ever". There will be an entirely new course for the running race, including a "Big Daddy Slide", whatever that is, thirty-five different "high quality, semi-permanent obstacles" plus "lots of mud and fun" for seven miles. Not sure how this represents a battle and less sure of where the fun comes into it, but there you have it.

*Tall towers*

From the feel of it, we are entering open fields and soon walking along the ridge of a hill. I don't remember climbing and have no reference point to measure against. It is still entirely white. Wendy has been having a mild panic attack for the past twenty minutes as it's only a guess that we're heading in the right direction. I have to admit, it's quite creepy being cut off from all sensations and at a complete loss as to where you are. I'm trying to keep her calm but am not feeling too chirpy myself. Disorientation is gripping the both of us.

If we guess right, we're in the vicinity of an old hill fort and from here apparently you have magnificent views of the giant Bristol Towers. Cabot's and Beckford's Towers dominate the Bristol skyline, with one standing 100 feet high, the other (Beckford's) towering one hundred thirty feet. Cabot's Tower was constructed in 1897 to commemorate John Cabot's voyage to America in 1497, a voyage in which he also managed to discover Newfoundland. Being wily, he decided to go with America and make his home there. Even today, Cabot is a big family name in that country, having merged with the Lodges back in the 19th century. The Cabot-Lodges did what all up and coming families do and entered politics, with Henry Cabot-Lodge becoming one of the country's most famous senators, and also the most educated, gaining his PhD from Harvard. But it is their wealth that defines them today, a family of what the Americans like to call "Bluebloods", who dominate social and political circles in many of the nation's cities.

Beckford's Tower was built a good deal earlier – 1827 – by William Beckford, an art collector, writer and spoilt, directionless son of a wealthy landowner. It was this unique 'folly' which he used as a hideaway to write his novels in seclusion and privacy. The tower was "shocking" to most who viewed it and was intended to be so. It's eight Gothic spires pierced the skyline and invited furious debate among onlookers. It took almost all of Beckford's inherited fortune and provided no return whatsoever, so a folly indeed. Beckford remained in the UK and unlike the Cabot-Lodges, did not go on to create a political and financial dynasty. In fact, he died relatively poor and unpopular from his extravagances.

If you read Tom Fort's excellent book - *The A303: Highway to the Sun* - you can gain a more salacious insight into the history of this tower. Before Beckford, the land, although not the tower, was occupied by the 2nd Earl of Castlehaven. He lived between 1593 and 1631, a short thirty-eight years. His life was cut short for a very obvious reason. When young, the fellow was married off to a daughter of another high profile and socially acceptable family but the two couldn't stand each other and went about pursuing their own interests, and it seems, desires. It turns out that the young Earl much preferred the company and intimacy of his equally young male servants. He would spend his days hunting, riding and frolicking with them and visiting their bedrooms at night. Because the Earl's wife was being deprived of his attention, he would often pay the male servants to sleep with her … and his step-daughter if they had time. It was an arrangement that seemed to make everyone happy.

As the story has it, when the master and his family weren't available the servants played among themselves. The problem was that they also liked to boast of their conquests outside the Earl's walls and as the tales of debauchery became more common and bawdier, the townsfolk became more unsettled. Eventually, the scandalised town leaders couldn't take it any more and gathered a bunch of the Earl's peers to sit in trial of his behaviour. They convicted him of rape and sodomy, charges which his own son brought against him, and sentenced him to beheading. Most of the servants were also rounded up and given various jail sentences for their crimes. Ever after, Fonthill Manor and the Earl were only ever spoken of in the most hushed of tones.

But today, without the scandal, both towers have more acceptable reputations as navigation points, landmarks, and curiously attractive symbols of Bristol's heritage. In addition to his other Cotswold treks JRR Tolkien spent quite a bit of his time wandering the hills and valleys around Bristol. He made copious notes about the landscapes and wove them into his most famous two books – *The Hobbit*, and *The Lord of the Rings*. A number of his names and places not only derive from Celtic and Saxon origins, but closely resemble places of this area. I like to think that he might have taken his idea for the Two Towers from the Bristol Towers, although there's no comparison between the beguiling city of Bristol and the darkness of Mordor.

# Bathing in Antiquity

At last, late in the afternoon, after many miles of drenched walking, we begin the final downhill run towards the realisation of a long-held mirage. There, in front of us, lie the outskirts of one of Britain's most beautiful cities. Bath is the end of the line for us and the Cotswold Trail. Two weeks ago, Wendy and I set off in high spirits from the charming village of Chipping Campden for what is officially a 102-mile walk. I think that with our various detours, wrong turns, doubling back and overnight stays well off the track we probably walked closer to 120 miles, but every one of them has been an adventure.

Now, as Bath comes into view four women join us on this last leg. They are all middle-aged, good friends, and meet each year to do a bit of a national trail. They have been walking the various parts of this trail for the past three years, in more manageable sections, usually over a period of three or four days. This trip has been a four-day one, which is a bit of a marvel as we notice that one of the women has a serious limp. It turns out that she is awaiting a hip replacement and is in agony with each step. I take my hat off to her for making it this far.

Our pace quickens as excitement builds for the climax of this walk and the poor woman with her defective hip is determined to keep up. The four of them talk a great deal and want to know about our extended trip through the UK. We learn that one is a university lecturer, one a "housewife", one a horse breeder and the other a professional seamstress. They are quite an eclectic bunch, and it seems their disparate professions have brought them closer together rather than having the *opposite* effect. We are all cheery despite the relentless rain and cold wind blowing right through our drenched clothing. Trees hang low with the weight of water, grass is slick under our feet, the distant streets are greasy wet and people hurry with heads down and umbrellas up. But our spirits remain high.

Wendy and I subtlety separate ourselves from the women as we enter the first streets with the excuse that we want to find a pub first. And we do. Heading along the first street, The King's Head shows itself in all its dry, warm, comforting splendour on our left. We pull open its outer door, duck our heads and are quickly inside. Dripping our way to the bar, creating pools of water on their clean, brown carpet, I ask if they have any hot soup.

"I'm sorry, we don't".

"OK, what about coffee?"

"No, sorry"

"Anything at all that's hot?"

"Sorry."


Being far too cold and miserable to order a beer I just ask the way to Bath Abbey. The barmaid explains that we are only a hundred yards from it, a short walk up the hill and there it will be, right in front of us. With spirits at a new high, off we go, arriving at a church within a couple of minutes. Alas, there is no way in all the fields of England that this church comes close to resembling Bath Abbey. It is simply another of the sixty-seven or so churches that populate the city.


The reason we specifically need Bath Abbey, is that it's where the walk officially ends, with a round Roman plaque embedded in the street to tell us so. Fortunately, another large group of walkers passes us. They are also finishing today, although we have no idea where they have come from. They confidently lead the way. The trail is still trying to extract as much pain as possible on this final, wet day. It continues to take us along narrow alley-ways, across several more fields, back down streets running parallel to those same alley-ways, past numerous other churches and finally, across Royal Victoria Park.

This, the largest and certainly grandest of Bath's parks, is luxurious, manicured, and filled with gardens and visitors. It's an exquisite setting, with the park stretching out in front of Bath's most sublime landmark – The Royal Crescent. This regal building is of fine Georgian architecture, constructed in 1774, and it's a struggle to keep its 500-foot length within your camera lens. Unbelievably, half the group we are following continues on its way, not giving this symbol of grand aesthetic beauty a second glance. Today, the building hosts thirty large, even palatial terrace houses. Let's just say that the very upper echelons of Bath society reside here and have done so for two-hundred and fifty years. The Crescent acquired its royal status after the Duke of York lived here on sabbatical for a period. Today it remains the single most identifiable symbol of Bath.

But it is not the end of the walk. On we trudge. By now, frustration levels are creeping up. Since entering Bath we have added at least another three miles on a path that is deliberately circuitous and unnecessary. Apparently, Tony Drake and Cyril Trenfield designed it this way so that Cotswold Way walkers could get a good look at the city before they finish. I'm not sure what sort of perverted sense of humour these fellows had. But you would think that by this stage of the walk, after 102 miles of dirt tracks, forests, fields with waist-high crops, steep hills and valleys, villages, wrong turns, false starts and steady rain as we have today, they would realise we've had enough for one day. That any such tours might be left for another day. No, apparently that didn't cross their minds.

It takes another mile and a half of frustration before we at last spot the magnificent Abbey ahead of us. Wendy and I still manage to walk a complete circuit of it before finding the Roman Stone embedded in the cobbles. A group of walkers is already there, huddled around and taking photos of each other. The stone contains names of towns and villages along the walk and is really a round, grey metal disc that is distinctly unprepossessing. Nevertheless, we ecstatically join in, stand on the stone, and furiously take photos of one another in the pouring rain, the results of which have us looking like very tired, drowned rats. By this stage Wendy is teary and emotional and I must say, we are both proud to have followed through with our quest and completed the entire journey.

Although the Roman disc is subtle, the Abbey certainly is not. It's a magnificent structure with the most intricate of architecture, great arched windows, turrets, buttresses, spires and vast sandstone walls. First founded in AD 675 as a simple religious house, the Abbey has since been transformed through numerous renovations and remodelling. Today, officially known as the Abbey Church of Saint Peter and Saint Paul, it represents one of the finest examples of Perpendicular Gothic architecture in Britain. It is definitely worth a tour, but *not* today.

*A most regal city*

Our time in Bath is limited and there is lots to see. First, we take the opportunity to visit another large supermarket. The bigger these supermarkets are, the more excited I get. I can't really explain this feeling or the resultant behaviour. I suppose I just like the idea of shopping for food and finding something different to add to that night's dinner. In Britain I've been particularly excited because there are so many more gluten free options than back home. There are also many more supermarkets that are so much larger. The major supermarket chains number ten, as well as four thousand Co-ops, plus several smaller chains in localised areas. The largest is Tesco, which controls about a quarter of the market, then come Sainsbury's, Adsa and Morrison's. At last count, all these added up to 10,308 stores nation-wide. That's a lot of people selling a lot of food. And I'm here to buy.

So, it's no surprise that spotting a large Sainsbury's this late in the afternoon brings on a serious level of excitement. My pace quickens as I begin to do a mental tally of what we'll need for dinner, despite numerous cautions from Wendy that this time we have to keep our shopping under control. With each supermarket visit so far, enthusiasm has got the better of me, so that we usually emerge with enough food for two or three nights rather than just the one. Wendy refuses to take food from place to place so a good percentage is always left behind.

Tonight, it's worse than ever. Somehow, we, or *I*, have managed to fill two shopping bags full of food for one night. There is chicken, broccoli, rice, mushrooms, cabbage, a bottle of sauce, aubergines, ham and cheese, lettuce and a loaf of bread for sandwiches next day, plus two packets of oat biscuits, a nice bottle of wine, a couple of beers, a bag of crisps and two desserts. Wendy looks at the food with horror, shakes her head and asks in her most sarcastic tone "So what happened to cutting back?" I shrug and try to give my most winning smile...which, as always, fails.

Did I not realise that the *room-only* B&B we are booked into tonight is just that, which means no kitchen? I have two bags of raw meat and vegetables and no way of cooking them. Wendy looks at me, shakes her head slowly; "Why don't you donate all our food to a local restaurant? Then we can have it served up to at hugely inflated prices". Sheepishly, I tuck the bags into the corner of the room, hoping they might just disappear of their own accord.

 Now it's time to get out of our drenched gear and into something warm and dry. And then off to celebrate, in a restaurant. We *do* feel like celebrating. Cleaned and dry and loaded up with an elegant, rather expensive Burgundy, Wendy and I head off in search of a suitably good restaurant in which to dine and reminisce. It's not long though, before our hunger takes over and the little pub we have now passed twice looks far more enticing than it should. Inside its pleasant if fairly non-descript. The menu is limited but what they have seems mouth-watering enough and TripAdvisor has given it a good rating. We're both ravenous and order far more than we could ever hope to get through. After the waitress takes the order we simply look at each other and shrug with a "you only live once" kind of attitude.

A full belly leads to an early night and long, dreamless sleep. Next day dawns with the rain of yesterday giving way to a bright, cloudless sky. Bath isn't just any city. It's a city that's arguably best known for its ties with the famous 18th and early 19th century novelist – Jane Austen. Best known for her classics such as *Pride and Prejudice, Emma, Sense and Sensibility, and Persuasion*, Austen was a powerful literary figure of her time. By some she is seen as a rather stifling romantic novelist, by others, a leading feminist of her time, structuring her novels around the unfortunate dependence of 19th century women on marriages advantageous to their social and economic welfare.

Her connection with the city of Bath is largely an unfavourable one, as her period here was also her least productive as an author. Given my own feelings about Austen, I don't necessarily see that as a blight on the city. I think perhaps Bath may have been a little too cosmopolitan and a little too progressive for the religious reserve of the Austen girls. What *is* significant, is that although she only graced the city with her presence for five years, until her father's death, her legacy is a lasting one. But time and distance from death usually mythologises a person's connection with place, and Bath Tourism has done a sterling job of milking her legacy for all it's worth. Each year, in order to capitalise on this masterstroke of literary luck, Bath hosts a Jane Austen Festival, with a full ten-day program of festival events featuring national and international stars from all walks of life. It's a PR orgy of self-promotion and exploitation and generates bucket-loads of money for the city. It's also only one of hundreds, if not thousands of Austen-related marketing exploits.

Bath, however, is about far more than a rather introspective novelist, although her significant talent must be acknowledged. Most date the history of Bath back to the Roman occupation, with the growth of a town around hot springs in AD 50-60. There are others who argue that its history actually stretches all the way back to 860BC, when King Lear's father caught the dreaded leprosy and was hidden away in the town until its hot springs could effect a cure, which failed to occur. This is probably playing around with local legends a bit too much. But given the ancient civilisations who roamed this general landscape it makes sense that Bath hosted some type of settlement long before the

Romans entered the scene. On their arrival, the Romans named Bath Aquae Sulis but many years previously in 750BC, the Celts had named it simply as Sulis, referring to the "waters of Sulis". About a thousand years later, the Saxons renamed it Hat Bathu, preferring it to be called after its hot springs. Whatever you like to call it, Bath has witnessed at least two and a half millennia of civilisation and despite a brief century or so beginning in the 1350s, when the plague wreaked its vengeance on the city and population fell by half, Bath has been known pretty consistently as a boom town.

As such a town, it has hosted its fair share of famous people. Other writers which, in my humble opinion are a good deal more entertaining than our beloved Austen have also made Bath home at one time or another. The likes of Charles Dickens, Henry Fielding and Mary Shelley, among others, have been inspired by this city and have written novels which have thrilled, provoked, frightened and led many a reader on their own journeys of discovery. In fact, Bath has produced greats from right across the cultural spectrum – actors Jonathon Hyde and Leo McKern, historian Sir Raymond Carr, and Black Books comedian Bill Bailey. A British Prime Minister by the name of William Pitt, one of my favourite musicians, Peter Gabriel, as well as the group

Tears for Fears, and a major character in our old school history texts, Horatio Nelson. The list goes on.

Doing what all newcomers to Bath do, we head out to visit the Roman Baths, which are located pretty well in the centre of the city. Despite their convoluted history they are a marvel to behold. The Roman museum below gives the visitor a brief glimpse into the lives and luxuries of an empire that invaded this tiny island two thousand years ago. They brought their customs, their knowledge and their thirst for all things indulgent, and made themselves completely at home for the next four hundred years. Within the museum there are thousands of Roman coins, gilt bronze statues, footwear, buckles, amulets, weapons and many of the belongings that accompany an empire of its size. It's a fascinating way to spend several hours of your time and we stay much longer than planned. There is also the Abbey that marked the end point of our journey to revisit, and the Crescent that symbolises the beauty of this city. Then we want to walk by the River Avon, which slices the city in two in its grand journey to the sea. It's a truly lovely river, bordered on each side by a walking trail so that you can stroll for miles along its banks, away from the bustle of the city and its throngs of people.

Two relaxing, blissful days are spent wandering the interest points of Bath. The walk is over, we don't have to wake at dawn and lift our packs anymore. Instead, we stroll, eat, and drink in the bewitching atmosphere of this place. We spend some time planning the next two months of our stay on this Island but most importantly, reflect on the magic that was the Cotswold Way.

## Final thoughts

What a feeling of achievement and deep contentment our walk has provided! We feel that the two weeks we have spent on this trail, are probably the most enjoyable, relaxed and profoundly uplifting two weeks of our lives. They have brought us even closer together. They have given us a deep and lasting appreciation for this land and its timeless history, and introduced us to a treasured way of life that is increasingly rare. We have laughed, learned, admired, wondered, been thrilled by, deeply touched by, and fallen in love with a delightful, storybook landscape and the people who inhabit it.

Along the way, previously held beliefs have faded, been replaced, been rejected. There is a new understanding of the fabric which holds communities together. How these villages and their folk fit within and complement this ancient landscape, is surprising and refreshing. Our journey has been physical but also metaphysical. At times, the wonder and magic of this exquisite region have almost overwhelmed. At others, they have simply seduced. I would say that if you only do one major walk in your life, make it this one.

# Notes

Burton, A., Cotswold way, Aurum Press, 2012

https://loghouseholidays.co.uk/quirky-facts-about-the-cotswolds/

Christie, M & Matthews, J. The economic and social value of walking in England. 2003, p.6

Click Liverpool,
http://www.clickliverpool.com/features/14212-10-fun-filled-facts-about-cheltenham-festival/

Bed and Breakfast.com
https://www.bedandbreakfast.com/info/about/history

Moffat, A. Britain: A Genetic Journey

https://annoyzview.wordpress.com/2012/02/23/where-is-boudiccas-grave/http://www.cheeserolling.com/p/cheese-rolling-trivia.html

http://www.english-heritage.org.uk/visit/places/great-witcombe-roman-villa/

http://www.learnenglishlanguagewell.com/2011/city-town-village-or-hamlet-differences/

https://www.differencebetween.com/difference-between-hamlet-and-vs-village/

http://www.3dgeography.co.uk/settlement-hierarchy

https://www.cotswolds.com/plan-your-trip/towns-and-villages/painswick-p670773

https://www.cambridge-news.co.uk/news/cambridge-news/ghost-ely-cromwell-video-orb-14158669
https://www.omlet.co.uk/guide/dogs/the_history_of_the_dog

https://www.cpre.org.uk/resources/housing-and-planning/housing/item/1939

https://www.wottonheritage.com/Lectures

https://www.nationaltrust.org.uk/horton-court/features/stories-of-the-past

https://mysodbury.co.uk/sodbury/old-sodbury-times
www.wow247.co.uk/2016/01/22/bizarre-facts-bristol/

(xviia)

https://www.telegraph.co.uk/news/uknews/1345980/Harry-Potter-and-the-source-of-inspiration.html

https://en.wikipedia.org/wiki/Brecon_Beacons

https://4adventurers.weebly.com/notes-on-the-national-parks/7-fun-facts-about-the-brecon-beacons-national-park

https://www.shponline.co.uk/stair-safety-day-25-facts-about-stair-safety/

https://www.statista.com/statistics/299155/number-of-stores-of-grocery-retailers-supermarkets-united-kingdom-uk/

https://gloscrimehistory.wordpress.com/2014/10/31/transported-to-a-better-life-joseph-pike-1829/

https://assets.publishing.service.gov.uk/governm
ent/uploads/system/uploads/attachment_data/fil
e/712317/AUK-2017-31may18.pdf

https://www.southglos.gov.uk/documents/leaflet
s/pte050032.pdf

https://en.wikipedia.org/wiki/Cold_Ashton

https://www.independent.co.uk/news/business/
news/uk-pubs-closing-at-a-rate-of-27-a-week-
camra-says-a6853686.html

https://www.thewi.org.uk/about-the-wi

https://theconversation.com/rural-pubs-really-
do-make-countryside-communities-happier-but-
they-are-closing-at-an-alarming-rate-72231

Fort, T. The *A303: Highway to the Sun*, Simon &
Schuster, 2012

http://www.localhistories.org/bath.html

66016753R00133